IMAGES
of America

LAKE MERRITT
JEWEL OF OAKLAND

This is an aerial view of Lake Merritt, the "Jewel of Oakland," as it is now, showing principal places and structures: A. Glen Echo Arm; B. Trestle Glen Arm; C. Bird Islands; D. Adams Point; E. Children's Fairyland; F. Lake Merritt Gardens; G. Kaiser Tower; H. Snow Park; I. Old City Boathouse, now Lake Merritt Chalet; J. downtown Oakland; K. Cameron-Stanford Mansion; L. Alameda County Courthouse; M. Oakland Auditorium; N. San Antonio Creek; O. Laney College; P. 1200 Lakeshore Apartments; Q. Old Boat Landing; R. Cleveland Cascade; and S. Pergola. (Google Earth.)

ON THE COVER: Lake Merritt is pictured at the Twelfth Street bridge in 1891 with sailboats and rowboats clustered around the boathouse. Boating has been a longtime recreation on Lake Merritt and remains popular today with sailing, rowing, and crew. (Oakland History Center, Oakland Public Library.)

IMAGES
of America

LAKE MERRITT
JEWEL OF OAKLAND

Jere H. Lipps

ARCADIA
PUBLISHING

Copyright © 2023 by Jere H. Lipps
ISBN 978-1-4671-0953-6

Published by Arcadia Publishing
Charleston, South Carolina

Printed in the United States of America

Library of Congress Control Number: 2023931757

For all general information, please contact Arcadia Publishing:
Telephone 843-853-2070
Fax 843-853-0044
E-mail sales@arcadiapublishing.com
For customer service and orders:
Toll-Free 1-888-313-2665

Visit us on the Internet at www.arcadiapublishing.com

CONTENTS

Acknowledgments   6

Introduction   7

1.   The Jewel   9

2.   Origins   31

3.   Americans   45

4.   Innovations   71

Bibliography   127

ACKNOWLEDGMENTS

Lake Merritt is part of Oakland's rich life and history. This book, a brief pictorial history of the lake, highlights selected people, structures, and events that loom large in that dynamic history. Many books, articles, libraries, and museums carry historical materials about the lake and Oakland. Online resources like Online Archive of California, Calisphere, Oakland History Facebook pages, lakemerritt.org, and Wikipedia.org provide quick access to various aspects of Lake Merritt's history. Ohlone websites provided information about the people who cared for thousands of years for the lands and the tidal estuary that became Lake Merritt. iNaturalist.org lists hundreds of species of the animals and plants of Lake Merritt. I am grateful for all of these resources and more, too numerous to note here, for the information I have absorbed. Some are noted in the image sources in this book, and selected books are listed in the bibliography on page 127. Most valuable and useful were the collections of Oakland History Center in the Oakland Public Library, 125 Fourteenth Street, Oakland, California, 94612. I thank the center's librarian Emily Foster for information, assistance with images and history, access, and permission to use historical materials that were essential to write this book.

This history resulted from studies started in 2001 by Dr. Kenneth Finger (University of California, Berkeley, retired) and me on Lake Merritt's microbiota. The history of the lake is important in understanding the development and history of its biota. That historical research, and more, led to this book. I thank Dr. Finger for his untiring efforts on the lake, in the lab, and in the study. I also thank Dr. James Carleton (professor, Williams College) who informed our biological studies since 2002. He also first stimulated my interest in Lake Merritt while he was a student at the University of California, Davis, when he told me about his work at the lake in the late 1960s. Dr. Carlton generously shared his data and images. I thank Dr. Michele Weber and Dawn Peterson for assistance in the field. Dr. Michael Kozuch, geologist, flew his drone to capture images around the lake that helped me understand various aspects of it, and I thank him for the use of his images. Katie Noonan, biologist, of the Rotary Nature Center Friends at Lake Merritt, provided information on the lake's biology, assisted by email and phone, and allowed use of her images. David Wofford, also of the Rotary Nature Center Friends at Lake Merritt, provided information on the eagle totem pole and the lake. James Covel sent me images and information about his late father, Paul Covel. Joy Hartnett emailed me information and images taken in the 1960s by her father, Jack H. Hartnett. Damon Tighe, naturalist and photographer, furnished images of the fish die-off in August 2022 at Lake Merritt, and Jim Roach, photographer, supplied photographs of birds and scenes at the lake. Eileen Delgadillo reviewed sections on the indigenous Ohlone people. Andrew Aldan, geologist, blogger, and writer, gave me advance access to his new book about Oakland's geology, provided images, and confirmed information. Aldan's book (2023) tells a comprehensive story of Lake Merritt's geologic origin, history, and physical setting. I thank all these people for their help, images, information, and other considerations.

INTRODUCTION

Lake Merritt is a beautiful lake embedded in the center of the city of Oakland, California. It has always been an inspiration for innovation as various visionaries from the Ohlone to modern people dealt with its dynamic waters. Today, it is a wonderful place for people to enjoy, play, recreate, and learn. The lake serves the diverse Oakland population of over 440,000, who originated from all continents and many islands. It is a unique environment for these people, their children, animals (especially birds), and plants in this city and the East Bay.

Today's Lake Merritt is an estuary formed by complex interactions of geology, oceanography, biology, and people over a long history reaching back into the ice ages more than a million years ago. Except for two short times, the sea was lower than it is now, and neither San Francisco Bay nor Lake Merritt estuary existed. Instead, rivers and streams ran through the valleys that underlie the bay and Lake Merritt where they were seasonal, rapidly running streams. During two periods, the oceans rose from lower levels to today's sea level or above. The bay river valleys and the lower parts of Lake Merritt's streams were flooded, turning them into estuaries, mudflats, or marshes where sea and fresh waters mixed. The first of these periods took place from about 125,000 to 120,000 years ago, drowning the lower parts of the streams that formed the Lake Merritt estuary as well as flooding the region around the ancient bay as the sea rose about 27 feet higher than it is now. An estuary with mudflats and marshes formed as the water level rose and fell. The shoreline and deposits of this high sea stand occur at Lake Merritt and elsewhere around the bay and open coast. The sea again dropped to levels nearly 400 feet below current seas between 20,000 and 18,000 years ago as glaciers formed worldwide. At this time, the streams joined rivers, which then went through the Golden Gate and across a coastal plain to empty into the Pacific Ocean 30 miles west of the Golden Gate and nearly 400 feet lower than it is today. As the climate warmed, the glaciers collapsed or melted into the sea, raising the sea level to where it is now about 4,000 years ago. And once again, Lake Merritt became an estuary where the sea met the streams headed west. The floor of the streams began to accumulate sediment, forming the mudflats and marshes. Lake Merritt, as it is known today, is only about 4,000 years old.

During the last low stand of sea level between 20,000 and 13,000 years ago, people migrated from northeastern Asia (Siberia) to Alaska, walking across or boating along the Bering Land Bridge exposed by the lowered sea level. These people spread across North America, populating the continent; some arrived along the California coast at least 13,000 years ago. Once the sea penetrated the Golden Gate, people known as the Ohlone built over 425 large mounds of shells, mud, and sand around the bay. Those mounds had camps and villages on them where the people lived and died, and are considered sacred by the Ohlone today. The Chochenyo-speaking Ohlone Huichin people lived from Lake Merritt north to beyond Albany. The Huichin people lived by themselves for at least 3,700 years in the East Bay until the Spanish explored the San Francisco region in the 1700s. Missionaries arrived, establishing Mission San José in 1797. The Huichin were taken to this mission, converted to Catholicism, taught Spanish ways, and labored at the mission and on its lands with thousands of livestock. The Spanish brought diseases as well that devastated the Ohlone population. The Indigenous people lost their familial and tribal affinities as a result. In little more than 40 years, Mexico obtained independence from Spain and secularized the missions. It also recognized the land grants awarded to Spaniards, including the San Antonio Rancho of 44,800 acres in the East Bay. In the 1840s, Americans began to encroach onto the grant lands, resulting in the Mexican-American War from 1846 to 1848, with California and the

Southwest ceded to the United States. When gold was discovered in California's Sierra Nevada in 1848, Americans and gold seekers from elsewhere in the world rushed to San Francisco and then the goldfields in the mountains. Many of these would-be miners returned to the Bay Area and settled on lands owned by land grantees. California became a state in 1850, and in 1852, the town of Oakland was incorporated, with the city following in 1854. The tidal flats of the future Lake Merritt became a hazardous place where Oakland's waste and sewage was dumped from 1853 to 1890. Even so, certain people, like Samuel Merritt, an early resident and mayor of the city, could see the potential of the lake as a residential and recreational highlight. The city was growing and moving closer to the shores of the lake.

The Huichin at the same time were enslaved and mistreated. The State of California and its first governor, Peter Hardenman Burnett, who referred to Native Americans as "the Indian foe," promoted the extermination of natives with funding for militias and individuals to hunt them and remove them from their lands, and offered bounties of $5 for a body or scalp and 25¢ for an ear. This genocide took the lives of at least 16,000 Native Californians between 1840 and 1870. In 2019, Gov. Gavin Newsom apologized for California's genocide and mistreatment of Native Americans. However, exploitation, discrimination of all sorts, and violence still torment the Native Californians today.

The traditional, ancestral, and unceded land of the Huichin (xučyun) Ohlone people, and the successors of the sovereign Verona Band of Alameda County includes Lake Merritt, Oakland, Piedmont, and Berkeley. It was and continues to be of great importance to the Muwekma Ohlone Tribe and other familial descendants of the Verona Band. Article 12 of the United Nations Declaration on the rights of Indigenous peoples recognizes their "right to manifest, practice, develop and teach their spiritual and religious traditions, customs and ceremonies; [and] the right to maintain, protect, and have access in privacy to their religious and cultural sites." The Huichin and all the Ohlone deserve respect, consideration, and recognition by the modern citizens of the Bay Area for their presence, care, and dedication to Lake Merritt, where they lived for thousands of years.

Three men arrived in Oakland in 1849 or 1850. Horace Carpentier, Edson Adams, and Andrew Moon sold lots subdivided from the 160 acres acquired from Vincent Peralta. Oakland continued to grow from 1860 to 1900 (1,543 to 66,960 people) to become a major city in California, and as it grew, Lake Merritt became increasingly important to the city. The Intercontinental Railway connected the East to Oakland. Lake Merritt became the first nature reserve in the United States to protect chiefly birds but also all organisms. Merchants in San Francisco moved to Oakland, and these and other wealthy men built mansions at Lake Merritt. A religious school opened on its shores, and residents utilized the lake as a hunting ground for birds, for boating, and for swimming. In the early 1900s, Oakland was impacted by several pandemics and a major earthquake. Lake Merritt garnered attention with the installation of monuments and fountains along its edges. Later, big business came to the lake with the development of shoreline structures housing various enterprises, apartment buildings, colleges, churches, public boathouses, a museum, and county and city agencies. Educational facilities, the Rotary Nature Center, and the Lake Merritt Institute were established at the lake. The lake itself was stabilized to control flooding and odors and the erosion of the shorelines with rock armoring or concrete abutments. Its parks were established and manicured, and Children's Fairyland ensured that families would always be welcome at the lake. The lake was well on its way to becoming the Jewel of Oakland. Resting in the middle of a big city, the lake was not immune to problems such as pollution, trash, the unhoused, vandalism, theft, and violence on occasion. In the 2000s, city Measure DD was passed by 80 percent of the voters who provided funds ($198 million) for the completion of improvements to the lake including widening the channel to the bay, building trails, boat passageways, bridges, a recreation center and an arts center, land acquisition, and creek restoration. Lake Merritt is truly a jewel.

One

THE JEWEL

Lake Merritt lies in the middle of Oakland, a richly diverse city with a growing population of 440,600 adjacent to San Francisco Bay in Northern California. It is a unique estuarine, tidal water body. The lake and the surrounding land are part of the City of Oakland's park system. The entire lake is rimmed by paths and pleasant boulevards. Its western edge is adjacent to downtown Oakland, and on its eastern side lie residential areas chiefly comprised of apartment buildings. Along its northeastern edge and on Adams Point are Lakeside Park with Children's Fairyland, Lake Merritt Gardens, various monuments, and the Rotary Nature Center as well as other places for recreation and learning. To the southwest, Lake Merritt Channel leads from the lake to the Inner Harbor of Oakland and on to San Francisco Bay, all part of the winding estuaries along Oakland's shoreline. With a 3.4-mile circumference, an area of 140 acres, and a depth no greater than about 10 feet, the lake offers a peaceful setting where citizens can walk, run, play, boat, picnic, and watch and learn about wildlife, including a wide variety living in the lake itself. Families and school classes visit Lake Merritt to learn about plants and animals, the birds in particular; study some of the history of Oakland; and, most importantly, for recreation. After over 180 years of development and improvement of the lake, it is enjoyed by all the diverse people of the San Francisco Bay area and is truly the Jewel of Oakland.

Lake Merritt is a dynamic tidal lake embedded in the city of Oakland in a northeast-southwest direction with two arms at its northwestern and northeastern ends (top) where streams from the East Bay Hills enter. It is accessible from all sides by roads and paths winding through parklands. An estuary, the lake is connected by Lake Merritt Channel (center) through which the tides move twice a day between Oakland's Inner Harbor (bottom) and the lake. Because of these connections, the lake has variable temperatures and salinities that range from freshwater after heavy rains to nearly normal seawater when high tide brings water from the bay into the lake. Before 1868, the lake was known as San Antonio Slough with smelly mudflats and seagrass marshes exposed at low tide. It has changed in the last 155 years and is far more pleasant now. The natural marshes and mudflats are gone, islands have been added, and the shorelines stabilized with walls and pathways, making Lake Merritt a ready and desirable destination. (Google Earth.)

Lake Merritt, seen from the northeastern Trestle Glen Arm, shows its close relationship to the surrounding communities. The plants in the foreground decorate the shore at the Pergola. On the eastern side (left), residential buildings stand along Lakeshore Avenue with single homes on the hills overlooking the lake. At the western end, the tall 1200 Lakeshore Apartments (left), the Oakland Auditorium (center), the Oakland Museum of California (center right), and the Alameda Courthouse (right) are prominent landmarks. The lake's western edge (far right) abuts the city of Oakland's downtown, with public, office, and apartment buildings close to the lake and extending west and north into the city. Boulevards and pedestrian paths follow the lake's edge, while on the other side of the road, buildings overlook the lake. Empowerment Park and the Bird Islands are seen in the foreground at right. Farther out are a line of floats with birds across Trestle Glen Arm, and in the distance, a line of buoys extends across the lake from the Bird Islands to the eastern shore to keep boats from disturbing the birds. (Jim Roach.)

The western shore of Lake Merritt, seen from an altitude of 210 feet across Adams Point (bottom) and the Glen Echo Arm (center), is home to county, city, and private offices; upscale apartment buildings; a cathedral; and a park. A sliver of San Francisco Bay, the hills, and the city of San Francisco are visible in the distance (upper left to center). Downtown Oakland, established 171 years ago, is in the upper right with its large buildings. Lakeside Drive, together with a greenbelt and walking paths, runs along the lake. On the left are the Alameda County Courthouse, the Oakland Public Library, the Cameron-Stanford Mansion in the trees, and the former boathouse, now Lake Chalet Restaurant, at the water's edge. The curved structure at center is the Kaiser Tower, a 28-story building dominating the view in Glen Echo Arm. This area was revitalized by new construction on sites where mansions and colleges formerly stood. The Lake Merritt Boating Center and Adams Point are seen at bottom. (Michael Kozuch.)

The northwestern branch of Lake Merritt is called the Glen Echo Arm for the creek that enters at its apex at the intersection of Harrison Street and Grand Avenue. This arm, like the lake most everywhere, is less than 10 feet deep but rich in life. Across Grand Avenue (upper right) is the Veterans Memorial Building with memorials to veterans of the Spanish-American War and the torpedo portal of the USS *Maine*. Glen Echo Creek flows to the lake west of the Veterans Memorial Building. To the east on Adam's Point are Children's Fairyland (upper right), the Gardens at Lake Merritt, Bonsai Gardens, and the Mid-Century Monster play structure on the white beach. The western shore is notable for the Cathedral of Christ the Light (2008); the Ordway Building, a 28-story skyscraper that is home to Kaiser Permanente corporate offices; the curved Kaiser Tower, 26 stories tall; and the Lake Merritt Plaza office building and concert venue with Snow Park (1960) in front. The Regillus Apartment (1922) sits to the left of Snow Park. Adams Point is at bottom right, with the Children's Memorial barely visible. (Michael Kozuch.)

The southeast shore of Lake Merritt, formerly providing sites for houses and mansions, now sports an old boat landing (center), sitting areas, apartments (upper right), and views across the lake to Oakland's downtown and to both arms of the lake. At low tide, as seen here, the shallow lakebed is exposed. Lake Merritt Channel connects Oakland's harbor to this part of the lake, allowing the exchange of tidal waters and organisms. (Author photograph.)

The eastern shore of Lake Merritt has always been a desirable place to live. Large apartments were built to take advantage of the lake views. These apartment buildings are quite elegant, such as the 1200 Lakeshore Apartments building, opened in 1967, which sits prominently on the southeastern end of Lake Merritt. The building has 28 floors and a penthouse, housing high-end apartments and special facilities for the occupants. Many celebrities live there. (1200 Lakeshore Apartments.)

The northeastern shore of Lake Merritt ends between hills cut through by several creeks, forming Trestle Glen Arm. The shoreline is separated from the overlooking buildings by greenbelts, pathways, and Lakeshore Avenue. These shorelines are prime apartment locations along the boulevard, with homes in the hills. The Bird Islands (left), the Pergola and Eastshore Park (beyond the end of the arm), the Cleveland Cascade marked by the trees (center right), and Pine Knoll Park (far right) are popular attractions. The upper part of the arm is closed off by a line of buoys to protect the birds

from boats. Formerly, Lake Merritt extended through the area of Eastshore Park past the MacArthur Freeway. It is now the site of the Lakeview Branch of the Oakland Public Library, Astro Park play area, and a local vendor marketplace on weekends. Pine Knoll Park sits on three lots adjacent to Wayne Avenue and was donated to Oakland in 1907 by Emelie Chabot, the wife of Anthony Chabot's brother Remi, who had received a generous bequest in Anthony's will. (Michael Kozuch.)

Eight public parks lie around Lake Merritt, with three more on the Lake Merritt Channel. Most are well used by employees from businesses, families on weekends, and people looking for interesting places or just hangouts. Lakeside Park on Adams Point is the largest park; it contains a variety of places of interest. Empowerment Park is graced by trees and green grass and welcomes picnickers and families to organized events and vendors. (Author photograph.)

Within Lakeside Park are Children's Fairyland, perhaps the best-known attraction at Lake Merritt, and the gardens near Adams Point. The Bird Islands are best viewed from this park. Snow Park, on the west side of the lake, is a popular place to hang out. Peralta, Channel, and Estuary Parks are located along Lake Merritt Channel from near its connection with the lake to Oakland Harbor. (Author photograph.)

Lake Merritt Channel, previously San Antonio Creek, is in a complex of estuaries that form Lake Merritt, the Oakland Harbor, and the channel at Alameda Island, connected to San Francisco Bay, an estuary itself. These are tidal, allowing water and animals to flow inward on high tides and outward on low tides. The incoming water has a salinity between 75 to 90 percent of normal seawater. Freshwater delivered to the lake by three major streams, a number of drainpipes, and runoff floats on the denser saltwater. Like estuaries in general, the channel and lake vary greatly over time and place. The original width of the creek was constrained by filling in the wetlands along the shores, but recent modifications widened the creek, increasing the flow of water to the lake and making it more marine in its properties and biology. The creek supports a wide variety of wildlife. (Author photograph.)

The view from the foot of the Cleveland Cascade on the east shore of Lake Merritt encompasses the northern edge of the lake. On either side of the Cleveland Cascade are apartment buildings, but across Lakeshore Avenue and the Trestle Glen Arm are Empowerment Park, Lake Merritt Gardens, Adams Point, and the western Glen Echo Arm of the lake. Lakeshore Avenue is busy, but has parking. The paths and greenbelt extend around the lake, and vendors commonly sell their wares on the greenbelt. Two elegant condominium buildings, the Bellevue-Staten Building (right, 15 stories, constructed in 1929) and the Park Bellevue Tower (center, 25 stories with 152 units, erected in 1967), are on the northern side of the lake along with the Bird Islands, the Oakland Boating Center, and Adams Point (left). Lake Merritt Gardens are next to the Park Bellevue Tower, among the trees to its left. Beyond these, across Glen Echo Arm, are the Kaiser Tower (center, 26 floors, built in 1960), the Lake Merritt Plaza (left of Kaiser Tower, erected in 1985), and Snow Park in the trees in front of the plaza. (Author photograph.)

The paths that follow the 3.4 mile circumference of Lake Merritt are paved and mostly close to the water. People use these paths for walking, jogging, or talking, while others stroll with their babies underneath trees and the Necklace of Lights suspended from poles and lit at night. Nice views of the lake, the city of Oakland, and the landscapes beyond can be seen from most spots along the paths. Photographers delight in the views, water features, and animals. At low tide, the sand and rocks in the shallow water are exposed, along with shells of dead clams and snails scattered along the shore and filamentous green algae growing in the water. A close look may reveal a fish or two or a bird hunting and diving into the water. (Both, author photograph.)

Lake Merritt is well-known for the birds that permanently live there or visit the area. Both terrestrial and aquatic species can be seen on the water, grounds, and trees. The black-crowned night heron, one of five herons that call the lake home, was voted Oakland's Bird in 2019 at the suggestion of 12 third graders. The night heron lives permanently at the lake, in the neighborhoods, and in downtown Oakland. (Jim Roach.)

Two egrets occur at Lake Merritt, the American snowy egret with its black beak and the great egret with a yellow beak and larger size. This is a snowy egret hunting along the shore. Both species eat other animals, preferring fish, but they will take frogs, small mammals, crustaceans, reptiles, and other birds. They were hunted to near extinction in the 1850s–1860s but have made a comeback. (M. Granger.)

The Lake Merritt Amphitheater (left) lies on a grassy slope at the west end of the lake near Lake Merritt Channel. It is a nice venue for small performances and events of all sorts. Music and dance groups perform there as well as informal speakers hoping to gather a crowd. A gorgeous view down the length of the lake to its eastern end can be seen from the amphitheater. (Author photograph.)

This place also attracts both informal and school-supported activities for kids. School field trips instruct students on nature, birds, other animals, the lake, and local history. They assemble at the amphitheater for lessons and move from there to other spots near the lake, like the Cameron Stanford House. At low tide, sand, rocks, shells, and algae are exposed. (Author photograph.)

Programs for students have been offered at Lake Merritt at least since Paul Covel lectured to them in the 1950s (above). Others, independently organized, serve learners and interested people with exploration of the life in the lake by sampling and video to observe what animals and plants live there and their behavior, associations, and abundances. The students work in the field collecting data on salinity, oxygen content, temperature, and sediment as well as on plants and animals. It is a hands-on experience and the best way to teach biology and ecology of a wide variety of animals from every phylum to marine plants and microorganisms. Katie Noonan runs one of these programs at the lake. For safety during the pandemic, students wore masks in 2021. (Above, Jim Covel; below, Katie Noonan.)

The Cathedral of Christ the Light is reflected in the waters of the Glen Echo Arm of Lake Merritt. The cathedral was consecrated and dedicated by Bishop Allen Henry Vigneron on September 25, 2008, replacing the Cathedral of Saint Francis de Sales, which served as the Diocese of Oakland's cathedral from 1962 to 1989, when it was severely damaged by the Loma Prieta earthquake. (Library of Congress.)

A competition for the design of the cathedral was held, with the selection of Vesica Pisces ("Vessel of the Fish") by architect Craig W. Hartman as the winner. The cathedral, made of wood and glass, houses the spectacular church, various other facilities, and a mausoleum. A public plaza and a healing garden for survivors of clergy sexual abuse are outside the building on the grounds. (Library of Congress.)

The Bellevue-Staten Building, completed in 1929, is 15 stories high and contains luxurious, high-end condominiums. The building overlooks all of Lake Merritt, Empowerment Park, the Bird Islands, and Adams Point immediately in front of it and the city of Oakland in the distance from its location at the eastern end of the lake in the Adams Point neighborhood. The view at left is from the edge of the lake. The building boasts a two-story Art Deco lobby and a pool, exercise room, and sauna on the first floor. It contains 36 one- or two-bedroom condominiums up to 2,000 square feet in size. It was listed in the National Register of Historic Places on December 27, 1991. Below, from over 200 feet above the building, its unique Spanish Baroque and Art Deco style is clear. (Left, author photograph; below, Michael Kozuch.)

While the Lake Merritt shoreline seems to be lined with newer buildings, some older ones have been restored or repurposed. The Lake Chalet Restaurant, for example, occupies the old High Pressure Pumping Station No. 1, built in 1909 in response to the 1906 earthquake and fire in San Francisco. The City of Oakland feared future fires and had no other way to acquire water quickly. The pump house consisted of a single concrete building with a tile roof and verandas to which the city added wings in 1913 on each side to accommodate boating. The pump house gradually deteriorated, and in 1955, it was closed. The city, in need of office space, refashioned the main building that housed the pumps to accommodate the Oakland Department of Parks and Recreation. Boats continued to be stored in the wings, but the main building finally required restoration, and the recreation and parks offices were moved out. The structure was then restored with Oakland's Measure DD funds and opened again in 2009, and the Lake Chalet Restaurant moved in. The boathouse was designated Landmark 139 in 2005. (Author photograph.)

Boating, long a pastime on Lake Merritt, is still quite popular. Sailing, rowing, sculling, and other types of boating are common on the lake. To support these activities, boathouses and landings were constructed at places around the lake. Boating activities are now supported by the Oakland Boating Center at Adams Point. The center offers an introduction to canoeing, kayaking, pedal boating, whaleboat rowing, sunfish sailing, and dragon boating, as well as courses on boating, rentals, and pontoon boat tours, some especially for youth. Sculling activities are based at the municipal boathouse, now the Lake Chalet Restaurant, where shells are stored (below). From there, the Lake Merritt Rowing Club provides coaching and competition opportunities. Gondolas can be rented near the Lake Chalet Restaurant as well. Powerboats, although once allowed, are no longer permitted on the lake. (Both, author photograph.)

The curved Kaiser Center (left) and Kaiser Permanente (right) buildings dominate the Glen Echo Arm of Lake Merritt. They occupy 7.2 acres on the old College of Holy Names property, purchased by Kaiser in 1956 at Harrison Street where it curves as it meets Lakeside Drive. The Kaiser Center includes the 28-story, T-shaped Kaiser Tower, a large, curved building completed in 1960; the Kaiser Center Mall, a three-story office and retail edifice; and a five-story, 1,339-space parking structure with a 3.5-acre rooftop garden, which includes a park with a reflecting pond, wooden bridge, lawns, mature trees, and abundant seating. The Kaiser Tower housed Henry J. Kaiser's world headquarters and Kaiser's personal residence on the upper floors until he moved to San Francisco, as well as other businesses and offices of the president of the University of California. It was designed by Welton Beckett as a modern structure with views of Lake Merritt, San Francisco Bay and city, and the rooftop garden. The Kaiser Center is now owned and operated by the Swig Company of San Francisco. (Author photograph.)

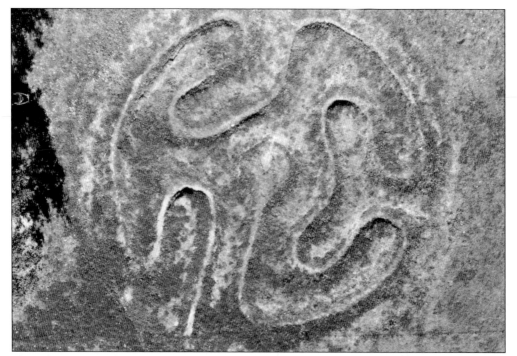

The Lake Merritt Labyrinth in the grass in Lakeside Park across from the Bird Islands is a circular structure 50 feet in diameter and built with raised ridges marking a 300-foot-long path spiraling into a central circle. Adults and children can walk or run through it or contemplate its possible spiritual qualities. Alex Champion, the artist who built it in 1992, earned a doctorate at UC Berkeley and in 1987 turned to sacred geometry and the construction of more than 100 sculptured gardens. The Oakland Department of Parks and Recreation commissioned and provided funding to build the labyrinth. The labyrinth fell into disrepair when weeds overgrew it, the path was degraded, and the ridges were worn down. In 2016, Carl Singer organized volunteers and rehabilitated it. Since then, it has been enjoyed by all. (Both, Michael Kozuch.)

Two

ORIGINS

Lake Merritt's origin can be traced back at least a million years when ice age glaciers waxed and waned, changing sea levels worldwide. Low sea levels occurred at cold times when glaciers were built from evaporated ocean water, and high stands formed at warm times when the glaciers crumbled or melted into the sea. Mostly, sea levels were too low to fill San Francisco Bay and San Antonio Slough, the future Lake Merritt. The bay and slough were river and stream valleys that joined and emptied into the ocean well beyond the Golden Gate. Only twice did the climate warm and the glaciers collapse and melt, increasing sea level to the present height or more. Between 125,000-120,000 years ago the sea rose almost 30 feet above today's level, eroding the shorelines to form terraces. From 20,000 years ago until about 10,000 years ago, sea levels stood at about 400 feet below the present level, creating a wide coastal plain some 30 miles wide that today lies under the sea off the Golden Gate. The oceans then rose 400 feet, flooding San Francisco river valleys to make the bay starting 8,000 years ago. The bay attained its current elevation and extent about 4,000 years ago.

During the last time the sea level was low, people crossed from Asia to North America on the Bering Land Bridge and migrated inland or down the coast to occupy California. For 13,000 years, these people lived undisturbed by any other humans, developing physically simple but socially complex civilizations filled with traditions based on tribal and familial affinities. As the sea filled the bay and its estuaries, the people followed the migrating shore, eventually living around the bay and estuaries on shell mounds they built. The people living around San Antonio Slough belonged to the Huichin group of the Ohlone people who occupied California from Monterey to the Carquinez Strait.

All this changed when Spanish explorers, soldiers, and missionaries discovered San Francisco Bay in the 1770s. The Ohlone were taken to the newly built missions to work in them and in the huge surrounding ranchos with livestock, disrupting traditions and networks. The Ohlone were decimated by incorporation into the Spanish and Christian strictures of the missions, by enslavement, and by introduced European diseases. Forty years later, Mexico won independence from Spain and ended mission life, although it was too late for the Ohlone to recapture life as they once knew it. Spaniards had been granted large ranchos, including Rancho San Antonio with 44,800 acres in the East Bay to Luís María Peralta. Peralta's four sons were each given a portion of the rancho with Vicente and Antonio Maria acquiring land around San Antonio Estuary, later known as Lake Merritt. The Mexican-American War from 1846 to 1848 resulted in Mexico ceding California and most of the Southwest to the United States in exchange for $15 million.

Lake Merritt sits in a complex of faults and folded rocks in the San Francisco Bay region, all part of the San Andreas fault system, the boundary between two tectonic plates. This map shows the major faults, the North American and Pacific Plate motions (arrows), and the approximate sites and years of major earthquakes that have affected Oakland and Lake Merritt. Smaller, less damaging earthquakes occur regularly on all the faults. Hills were pushed up along the faults between the Pacific Ocean and the Great Valley creating a valley where the modern bay lies. That valley filled with water as a river from an ancient lake in the San Joaquin Valley eroded through the hills northeast of the bay 620,000 years ago. The bay then emptied to the sea through Colima and only through the Golden Gate for the past few hundred thousand years. Mostly, the valley was dry because the sea level was lower than the Golden Gate. The San Antonio Slough developed as streams coming from the hills were flooded by rising seas. (Base map, US Geological Survey.)

Merritt Canyon, named by geologist Andrew Aldan, underlies Lake Merritt and its channel. The canyon was eroded by ancient creeks flowing from the hills during low sea levels in the past 800,000 years. The sea fell about 400 feet lower than it is now 20,000 to 18,000 years ago, and those creeks then cut a canyon 200–600 feet deep into the hills and coastal plain. At high sea levels, an estuary with mudflats and marshes formed, and sediment filled the canyon where the creeks coming out of the hills slowed and dropped their sedimentary load. When the next low stand of the sea occurred, those sediments were swept away, eliminating the history of previous times. The free-flowing parts of Glen Echo Creek (right) and the view down Sausal Creek near Park Boulevard from Leimert Bridge (below) provide a notion of what Merritt Canyon may have looked like thousands of years ago when sea level was lower. (Both, author photograph.)

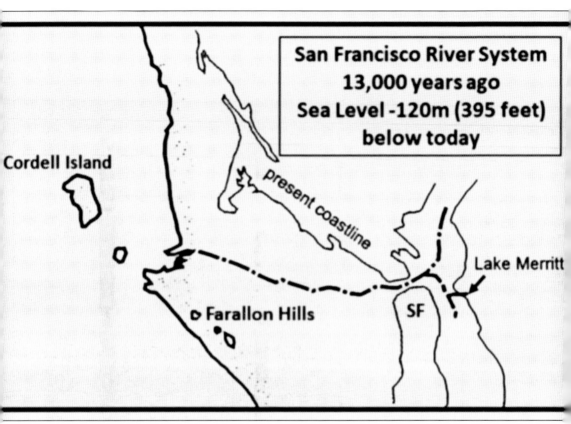

San Francisco River System 13,000 years ago Sea Level -120m (395 feet) below today

Cordell Island

present coastline

Lake Merritt

Farallon Hills

SF

Modern people, *Homo sapiens*, evolved about 200,000 years ago in Africa and spread to Europe and Asia, but not to the Americas. With the sea level as low as 400 feet (120 meters) below present from 18,000 to 10,000 years ago, people crossed the Bering Land Bridge from Asia into Alaska. They moved down the coast, likely in boats, and possibly in an ice-free corridor, arriving in California perhaps about 13,000 years ago. These people lived along the coast, 30 miles off today's shore (above), which is now up to 400 feet underwater, so their record is lost. The sea level rose as the glaciers and ice sheets collapsed and melted when the climate warmed, filling the river and stream valleys of the Bay Area. The people moved with the shoreline as seawater extended into the river systems of San Francisco Bay valley, approaching the present level about 4,000 years ago. The bay filled and its tributary streams flooded, forming a variety of estuaries, including the San Antonio Slough. The Ohlone people living along the bay's shores then built enormous shell mounds. (Author map.)

San Antonio Creek (pictured around 1900), now called Lake Merritt Channel, connects Lake Merritt to the Oakland Inner Harbor and San Francisco Bay. When seawater filled the bay about 4,000 years ago, the old river-cut canyons were drowned and sediments accumulated in them, filling in the streambed and forming estuaries with mudflats and marshes. San Antonio Creek and its tributaries coming from the East Bay hills formed a slough with saltwater inundating the mudflats and marshes at high tides and exposing them at low tides. The slough hosted abundant shellfish and fish, which were hunted by the Ohlone people living nearby on shell mounds they built with shells from animals in the slough. The slough took on smells of decomposing algae, shellfish, and microorganisms, and that process used up the oxygen in the water, occasionally causing the death of organisms living on or near the bottom. San Antonio Creek and San Antonio Slough, now called Lake Merritt, are known as estuaries as they experience inflow of seawater and of marine animals and plants from the San Francisco Bay. (Oakland History Center, Oakland Public Library.)

The San Antonio estuary formed when the sea invaded the lower reaches of the streams, including their mouths and the convergence of three main streams. Freshwater mixed with marine water as the oceans rose worldwide. The lake's watershed (4,650 acres) includes Glen Echo, Trestle Glen, and Park Creeks and tributaries that flow from the East Bay hills through the estuary and San Antonio Channel to San Francisco Bay. They flowed freely until modern times. Parts of Glen Echo still flow in open channels above Lake Merritt and close to Broadway Avenue (shown above at flood stage in 2022 where it passes into the lake), but other parts are sent through culverts (below, on Glen Echo). Trestle Glen Creek has not flowed freely for decades as it was diverted completely to culverts. (Above, Adrian Cotter; below, author photograph.)

Ice age animals, the megafauna, lived in the East Bay, roaming the flats, canyons, and hills of the area for thousands of years, as in this illustration by William Huff. When the San Antonio Slough formed, these animals surely wandered along its shore. Humans living then would have interacted with them. The megafauna died out approximately 10,000 years ago due in part to being hunted. (University of California Museum of Paleontology.)

The megafauna was surprisingly different from animals today. Sabretooth cats, mammoths, ground sloths, American lions, dire wolves, California grizzly bears, and giant vultures, among others, occurred throughout California. Their fossils are abundant in deposits in the Irvington District of nearby Fremont. These "Boy Paleontologists" featured in the December 1945 *Life* magazine excavated and collected over 20,000 fossils that now reside at the University of California Museum of Paleontology. (Math-Science Nucleus.)

From approximately 8,000 to 4,000 years ago, the Indigenous milling stone people lived by San Francisco Bay, although their record was mostly lost due to sea level changes and construction after 1849. Since about 4,000 years ago, the Ohlone people left an elaborate record of their lives. They were well organized geographically by language and tribes, living in villages from the coast to the hills. They built more than 425 shell mounds around the bay from which the remains of villages, hundreds of burials, a myriad of tools, other artifacts, and their foods are known. The bay and land provided a bounty of marine shellfish, birds, and mammals as well as land animals such as deer and rabbits, and plants like acorns, grasses, and berries. While they may have burned the landscape to promote growth of desirable plants and animals, they did not farm directly. Reed boats like the one seen here in an 1822 painting by Louis Choris were used to fish, hunt, and clam in the bay and estuaries and perhaps to access the mounds at high tides. (National Park Service.)

Estimates of Indigenous people living in the San Francisco Bay region when the Spanish arrived in 1769 vary from 20,000 to 100,000. Perhaps half lived in the East Bay in Chochenyo-speaking Ohlone tribes. One group, the Huichin, lived near the San Antonio estuary north to beyond Albany, building shell mounds along the bay and streams of East Bay. Max Uhle mapped the mounds in 1902; the Xs indicate mound sites now known. (Author map.)

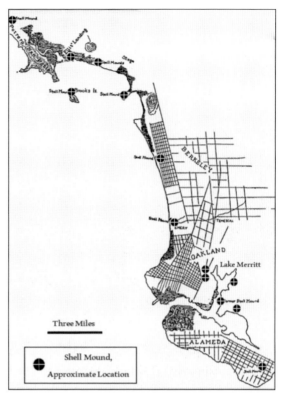

Mounds existed near the San Antonio Slough, San Antonio Creek, just east of Lake Merritt, in Oakland, at Clinton south of the lake, and on Alameda Island—all were destroyed by development before they were investigated. Many Huichin lived around the slough, where they harvested food. These mounds likely contained burials, tools, and assorted artifacts like those recorded at the Emeryville or West Berkeley mounds (pictured). (Oakland History Center, Oakland Public Library.)

39

ESTERO.

Brazo

Bosque, que
está al estsudes:
e de la Boca del Puerto

Brazo

Spanish missionaries and military explored the San Francisco region from 1769 through 1777. In 1772, close to the mudflats and seagrass of the San Antonio Slough, Franciscan friar Juan Crespi celebrated the first Catholic Mass in the region. The Spanish wished to colonize the area due in part to the presence of Russian settlements farther north. This Oakland area map, drawn by Pedro Font on the Anza Expedition of 1776 (north is to the right), shows in the upper part of the San Francisco Bay (*estero* or "estuary") some islands and rocks (Yerba Buena, Blossom, Alcatraz, and Angel) and the Golden Gate (*boca* or "mouth"). Alameda with the oak trees (center) bears the Spanish label "Forest that grows at the mouth of the port." The San Lorenzo estuary (left, *brazo* or "arm") is south of Alameda, and the Oakland estuaries are to the north. One of these branches is San Antonio estuary and San Antonio Slough. Oakland would arise north of the estuaries. The Huichin people lived in most of these places. (National Park Service.)

Father Serra, a Franciscan, came to Alta California in 1769 to establish missions and secure the land. Near the San Francisco Bay, Mission San José was founded in June 1797. Ohlone, mostly Huichin people, were taken to the mission and enslaved to work as laborers, farmers, cattlemen, and servants. Taught Christianity and Spanish culture, the Ohlone tribal and familial traditions were obliterated by the treatment they received at the mission. (Library of Congress.)

A pre-1933 headstone in the Ohlone Cemetery on an ancient village site near Mission San José marks the grave of 4,000 Ohlone who died of disease or labor at the mission. Today, people whose ancestors lived there belong to the Ohlone Muwekma tribe. Although they cannot know their tribal or familial affinities, they know their ways and sacred places passed down by oral traditions. (Library of Congress.)

The Spanish government awarded substantial land grants in California to military leaders and prominent citizens to reward them for their service. In 1820, Pablo Vicente de Solá, the last governor of Spanish California, granted 44,800 East Bay acres to Luís María Peralta for his 40 years of military service. Named El Rancho de San Antonio, the grant extended from present-day San Leandro north to Richmond. San Antonio estuary and Oakland were in the center of the grant. Thousands of cattle and horses were also included. The grants were honored by Mexico after its independence in 1821. In 1842, the rancho was divided between Luís Peralta's four sons. Vicente and Antonio Maria received land that included San Antonio Slough and estuary (shown here in part of a map of the East Bay area made by an artist in the Works Progress Administration in 1936). Each son built a home, raised livestock, and farmed on their land. They had little defense against American settlers squatting on their vast estates. (National Park Service.)

Mexico won independence from Spain in 1821, resulting in the First Mexican Empire, which secularized the missions and gave them to the Ohlone, as the missionaries intended. The Ohlone never had control of their lands due to Spanish land grants, recognized by the Mexican government, and American squatters who simply took possession of the land. Vicente Maria Peralta continued to raise cattle and other livestock, farm, and cut redwoods in the hills above his rancho, as did his brother Antonio, whose adobe built in 1840 was destroyed in the 1868 earthquake (pictured). The San Antonio Slough was used at high tide to move lumber and other commerce to San Francisco Bay and for hunting birds. (Oakland History Center, Oakland Public Library.)

Col. JOHN C. FREMONT,
REPUBLICAN CANDIDATE FOR PRESIDENT OF THE UNITED STATES.

Many Americans believed the United States had dominion over all of North America and that it should expand democracy and capitalism to the Pacific Ocean. John C. Fremont (1813–1890) led four expeditions in California from 1844 to 1853 during which his forces massacred hundreds of Indigenous people in Northern California. Fremont, a leader in the Mexican-American War from 1846 to 1848, defeated Mexican forces at Monterey, the capital of Alta California, and at Los Angeles. On February 2, 1848, Mexico ceded Alta California and the Southwest to the United States under the Treaty of Guadalupe Hidalgo. Just before the end of the war, gold was discovered in the Sierra Nevada, starting the Gold Rush of 1849. When California became a state in 1850, Fremont was elected a US senator. He was nominated as the first Republican candidate for president of the United States in 1856. This political poster shows him in Western garb on a horse, with mountains and men behind him, highlighting his achievements in the West. He lost the election to Democrat James Buchanan. (Library of Congress.)

44

Three

AMERICANS

Americans slowly moved into Mexican territory before the Mexican-American War. Some logged redwood trees in the Oakland hills until gold was discovered in the Sierra Nevada in 1848. By 1849, hopeful miners arrived in San Francisco preparing to prospect in the mountains. California became a state in 1850 and began a campaign to eliminate the Native Americans. The Ohlone, on whose land Oakland and Lake Merritt lay, had to claim they were Mexicans and lay low to avoid being killed. Failed gold seekers returned to San Francisco and started life anew. Perhaps 100 returned to the hills to clear-cut the redwood forests, destroying the last of the truly magnificent trees. These supplied the lumber and shingles used to build the growing cities nearby. Several men settled in the Oakland area in 1849–1850, followed by others, including, around 1850, Chinese who were escaping wars in China. They were discriminated against by the white community but worked in the fields and on railroads. Oakland was incorporated as a town in 1852 and as a city in 1854. When more people arrived, sewage was dumped into the estuary, causing odor problems for the residents moving near it. A dam was constructed in early 1869 to contain water in the slough and stop the smells. While the dam worked, the smells continued until sewage lines were constructed to take waste into San Francisco Bay. The lake's shores were subdivided into lots for the wealthy, and many of the founders of well-known businesses made their homes at Lake Merritt.

Lake Merritt, of course, is the most recent name for the estuary next to the city of Oakland. The first people who lived at the estuary, perhaps as long as 8,000 years ago, are unknown, but later, the Ohlone Huichin people who built shell mounds there about 4,000 years ago surely had names for it; however, those are lost to history. During Mexican times when it was part of Rancho San Antonio, it was called San Antonio Slough or Estero Peralta. When Americans moved in, they called it Peralta Lake or Indian Slough. Sometimes, they called it "the lake of 1,000 smells" due to its marshes, mudflats, and sewage. Samuel Merritt, fed up with the smells while mayor of Oakland, constructed a dam across San Antonio Creek at Twelfth Street. The dam changed the slough into a more pleasant lake by retaining high-tide water, thus eliminating the mudflats and marshes. Merritt donated the lake to the people of Oakland, who then called it Merritt's Lake and, in 1874, Lake Merritt.

Americans were in California at Sonoma in 1846, where they agitated for independence as the California Bear Republic. The republic lasted a mere 25 days, but its flag became a symbol for California. In 1911, a new bear flag was adopted with a California grizzly emblazoned on it. The last grizzly was killed in 1922, making California the only state with an extinct animal on its flag and seal, as well as the state animal. Not until gold was discovered in the Sierra Nevada Mountains in 1848 did Americans and gold seekers from other countries flock to San Francisco and then the goldfields. Among those who came to California were men who opened businesses in San Francisco and later moved across the bay to Oakland. As the forty-niners returned from their failed search for gold and settled in the San Francisco region, some clear-cut the magnificent coastal redwood groves above Oakland, sawed them into lumber, and shipped them through the San Antonio Slough. The sawmill shown here in Palo Seco Canyon in the 1880s was used to process the redwoods until the 1860s, when the last ones were cut. (Oakland History Center, Oakland Public Library.)

Moses Chase (1806–1891) arrived in the Oakland area in 1849. He had come to California from Boston, Massachusetts, sailing on board the *Capitol* around Cape Horn, leaving behind his second wife, Mary Ellen Clinton. Chase went to prospect for gold in the Sierra Nevada, but after six months on the Feather River panning for gold, he returned to San Francisco. He then crossed the bay to Oakland. At first, he lived in a tent near the future site of the Oakland waterfront and later moved to a house he built along the southeastern side of the San Antonio Creek downstream of the slough. The house was near present Eighth Street and Fourth Avenue on property now owned by Laney College. Chase and the three Patten brothers leased 160 acres southeast of the slough from Antonio Peralta after some quibbling. They subdivided the land into lots, and Chase incorporated Clinton, which he named for his wife who had passed away earlier while he was in California. (Oakland History Center, Oakland Public Library.)

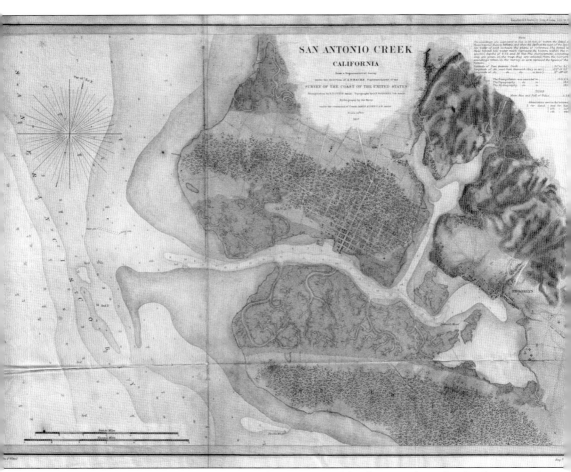

This 1857 map of San Antonio Creek and the town of Oakland was made under the direction of A.D. Bache as part of the United States Coast Survey. Oakland, incorporated as a town in 1852 and later as a city in 1854, was five years old when the map was issued, with a population of around 1,500 and growing rapidly. San Antonio Creek at that time included the tidal channel from the San Francisco Bay southwest of Oakland and the tidal channel and slough east of Oakland. The channel connected the San Antonio Slough, which ended in tidal marshes and mudflats on the northeast that in 17 years would be named Lake Merritt. The tidal channel directly southwest of Oakland later became Oakland Harbor, extending past Alameda, which then became an island. Hills, consisting of alluvial fan deposits, sloped upward preventing salty water from penetrating farther east. Such estuaries commonly smell bad as plants and animals die, a characteristic that would play a role in the making of Lake Merritt. (National Oceanic and Atmospheric Administration, Historical Map and Chart Collection, Office of Coast Survey.)

The Twelfth Street Bridge over San Antonio Creek is shown in 1884 where it enters the west end of the Lake Merritt estuary. It was built in 1852 by Horace Carpentier, an original resident of Oakland and its first mayor. The city could not pay him, so he made it a toll bridge to reach the towns developing east of Lake Merritt. The citizens in the 1860s, especially those living in mansions along the estuary, were upset by the smelly conditions produced by sewage, garbage, and junk dumped there. It was an unsightly open sewer with bad smells. Samuel Merritt built a dam at the Twelfth Street Bridge; water at high tide would flow into the estuary, covering the marshes and mudflats, and only some would flow back out at low tide. Enough would be retained to form a lake that would clean the estuary. Merritt finished the dam in 1869, but the estuary and tidal channel to the bay remained befouled into the 1900s as sewage and debris accumulated in it. (Oakland History Center, Oakland Public Library.)

Merritt's Lake, so-called from 1869 to 1874, remained undeveloped without rows of houses or trees and with weedy and muddy shorelines in the late 1860s and early 1870s. Cows grazed on the land around the lake. Even with its smells, the lake was a desirable place to live. Well-to-do men built houses along the lake, but in the mid-1870s, construction of mansions, led by Samuel Merritt, began on the west side. Property boundaries extended to the lake's edges. Roads and paths around the lake were developed later. In the 1880s and 1890s, Lake Merritt, as it was called after 1874, came under human management with dredging, roads, and the desire of the City of Oakland to make the lake a place for all residents to enjoy. (Both, Oakland History Center, Oakland Public Library.)

Edson Adams (1824–1888), along with Horace W. Carpentier and Andrew Moon, founded Oakland in the early 1850s. Born in Connecticut, Adams arrived in San Francisco in 1849 to search for gold in the Sierra Nevada. He returned from the goldfields and came to the Oakland area in 1850. He acquired 160 acres along what would become Broadway from Vicente Peralta. Nevertheless, Adams, Carpentier (first mayor of Oakland), and Moon sold lots illegally to the people coming to Oakland. Peralta later sued to repossess his land or receive payment, without satisfaction. In 1851, the three men hired Julius Kellersberger, a Swiss engineer who came in the Gold Rush, to survey Oakland for streets. In 1853, Kellersberger was made Oakland's engineer, and in the next year was elected the first engineer of Oakland. Naturally, Adams and his colleagues received choice parcels. Adams took the point of land extending into San Antonio Slough, a neighborhood that today bears his name. Adams's son Edson F. inherited the land and held onto it for decades. (Oakland History Center, Oakland Public Library.)

Samuel Merritt (1822–1890) came to Oakland in 1863 with the intention of developing the land and city. He was born in Maine and graduated from Bowdoin College with a degree in medicine at age 22. Interested in ships, he bought the brig *Reindeer* in 1849 with money borrowed from his brother and went to California to seek gold. He carried a letter from statesman Daniel Webster introducing him to Webster's friends in San Francisco. Arriving at San Francisco in 1850, Merritt sold the goods he carried for a significant profit and established a medical practice. Two years later, he purchased land along San Antonio Slough near developing Oakland. Merritt moved there in 1863 and opened construction supply businesses used by builders in the new town. Well known in Oakland, Merritt was the 13th mayor (1867–1869); he settled land disputes, made Oakland the terminus for the transcontinental railroad, and built a dam across San Antonio Creek. In 1868, Merritt was appointed a founding regent of the new University of California, a position he held until 1874. (Oakland History Center, Oakland Public Library.)

Oakland had become a railroad center for the West Coast, starting as the end point of the transcontinental railroad or Pacific Railroad that linked the area to the rest of the country. Constructed from 1863 to 1869, the railroad brought people and materials to the Bay Area. Extensions completed the route to the southern parts of the state. At San Antonio Creek, shown here at its entrance to Oakland Harbor in 1870, a trestle for the transcontinental railroad was built across the creek; large sailing ships are visible in the harbor beyond the trestle. A map of Lake Merritt in 1889 shows the Eighth Street and Twelfth Street Bridges that cross San Antonio Creek nearest the lake for local traffic to areas just southeast of the lake and two railroad bridges that cross the creek closer to the outlet into Oakland Harbor that continued the routes to the south. (Oakland History Center, Oakland Public Library.)

Development around Lake Merritt in 1869 was just beginning as prominent men began to develop the lake margins as integral residential parts of Oakland. This map shows that Dr. Merritt had a homesite in the northwest; E. Adams, a founder of Oakland, had property on the eastern point of land now named Adams Point and extending farther east into the hill; and Charles Newton, a merchant, owned 70 acres on the eastern lakeside between present-day Eighteenth Street to about Brooklyn Avenue. Merritt owned most of the property on the western side of the lake, which he sold or built homes on. Notable features are the Twelfth Street Bridge over San Antonio Creek, the dam built by Merritt just north of the bridge, and a bridge across the Glen Echo Arm of the lake. Lake Merritt had just been formed as a result of the dam. No official name is shown for the lake. In the downtown area along the western side, blocks are laid out in checkerboard patterns. (Author's collection.)

Anthony Chabot (1813–1888), an adventurous man born on a farm in Quebec, Canada, left for New York City, the Carolinas, and the Mississippi Valley as a young man and made a fortune. He departed to San Francisco and the goldfields in 1849. There, he originated hydraulic mining techniques, honing his skills in water transportation. He returned to San Francisco and inserted himself in the water supply business for that city. In 1865, Chabot discovered Oakland and accepted an invitation to be president of the Oakland Gas Company in 1866. He resigned within a year because he wanted to develop water supplies and distribution to the new cities of the East Bay, including Oakland, where he became known as the "Water King." Chabot built dams in the East Bay hills and distribution systems to supply water to Oakland, but he never engaged with Lake Merritt due to its estuarine salinities. In 1870, he extended the water supply to the other side of Lake Merritt, serving Brooklyn, a town later included in Oakland. (Oakland History Center, Oakland Public Library.)

This cottage alongside Lake Merritt's northeastern arm on First Avenue was said to have been Anthony Chabot's first home in Oakland. That may be untrue. His biographer, Sherwood D. Burgess, reports that Chabot lived in hotels in San Francisco and Oakland from 1866 to 1880, then moved to a house on Fourth Avenue in Oakland until he built his elegant home on the southeastern edge of Lake Merritt in 1881, as seen in the next image. (Oakland History Center, Oakland Public Library.)

In 1882, Anthony Chabot's home on Lake Merritt was completed near the intersection of First Avenue and East Fifteenth Street. His wife, Mary Ann, joyfully joined him in the new house but only for five years, as Chabot died on January 6, 1888. His wife lived in the house until 1904. It was razed in 1951. (Oakland History Center, Oakland Public Library.)

Lake Merritt lies less than three miles west of the Hayward Fault, which defines much of the geology and topography of Oakland as it slices through the eastern part of town. It moves continually, with small earthquakes occurring commonly. It also has had large earthquakes. The largest happened on October 10, 1868, estimated at magnitude 6.3 to 6.7. Its epicenter was near the town of Hayward, but it still disrupted the lives of 260,000 East Bay residents, killing 30 people around the bay. Structures from Hayward to beyond Oakland were severely damaged or destroyed, like the Alameda County Courthouse (pictured), constructed in 1857 in nearby San Leandro; Mission San José, built in 1797; and the Peralta home, built in 1840. Oakland and Lake Merritt were shaken badly, with people and horses running in the streets. The lake was not reported to have damage, although it was undeveloped and could have experienced slumping along the shores. The fault will produce similar large earthquakes in the future. (Bancroft Library.)

Samuel Merritt had interests besides the development of Lake Merritt. He was involved in bringing the transcontinental railroad to Oakland and the construction of the first buildings at the new University of California; he aimed to build a medical university in Oakland, which was accomplished after his death; and he had a love of the sea. When he came to California, he did so on his own ship. His passion for seafaring resurfaced in 1878, so he built the 72-ton keel schooner *Casco* based on his own plans. The ship was chartered by Robert Louis Stevenson for his cruise to the South Pacific in the last half of 1888, as shown here. In August 1890, Merritt sailed *Casco* across San Francisco Bay to Sausalito—his last trip, as he was forced to return to Oakland due to illness and died later that month. (Oakland History Center, Oakland Public Library.)

A group of six Sisters of the Holy Names of Jesus and Mary, a teaching order from Montreal, Canada, founded the Convent of Our Lady of the Sacred Heart in 1868, shown here on the shore of the Glen Echo Arm of Lake Merritt. The Sisters provided an education chiefly to the poor. They were invited by Fr. Michael King, pastor of Saint Mary's Church, to Oakland to build a school that offered a liberal arts and professional program for girls and teachers. They traveled a perilous route by ship to Panama, crossed the isthmus, and boarded another ship to San Francisco, where they arrived on May 10, 1868. Upon arrival, they were served strawberries and cream by Sisters of Mercy and Father King, starting a tradition celebrated as Founders Day with strawberries and cream still served by the Sisters every year. The convent was renamed College of Holy Names in 1908, Holy Names College in 1971, and Holy Names University in 2004. It was a fully accredited, Roman Catholic university. (Society of California Pioneers.)

The Convent of Our Lady of the Sacred Heart was established by the young Sisters Salome, Celestine, Marceline, Seraphine, Cyrille, and Anthony. From its start in 1868 as a developing liberal arts and professional school in a town with about 8,000 people surrounded by virtual wilderness, it enrolled only women. Graduates are shown here in 1890; like previous and later graduates, they went on to serve Oakland and the East Bay in education, business, and government positions. In 1955, the school opened a graduate school and admitted men. Although the school thrived at Lake Merritt, the property was sold in 1956 to Henry J. Kaiser for his Kaiser Center. The college then moved to 60 acres in the Oakland hills, starting classes in February 1957. At Holy Names College, the undergraduate programs continued to produce thousands of well-educated women and men. However, after the COVID pandemic and with increased financial woes, the university decided to close in May 2023 after 155 successful years. (Oakland History Center, Oakland Public Library.)

Lake Merritt and the San Antonio Creek blocked travel on the coastal plain from the hills to the bay, being too rugged for most travelers. Bridges for vehicles, railroads, and pedestrians were increasingly important as towns on the eastern side of the water grew and became important auxiliaries to Oakland. The Twelfth Street Bridge, a toll bridge built by the first mayor of Oakland, was the only way to move from Oakland to those towns. Travelers objected to the tolls and proposed that the city finance another bridge as an alternative. This new bridge at Eighth Street over the San Antonio Creek was built and became immediately popular with travelers to businesses and residents on the eastern side of Lake Merritt. The bridge is shown here in 1892 with an East Oakland Street Railway Company electric car crossing over San Antonio Creek to the east side of the lake. (Oakland History Center, Oakland Public Library.)

Merritt's Lake, as it was once known, was a tidal estuary connected to San Francisco Bay. As a result, animals and plants invaded it from the bay. Fish, shellfish, and other marine animals lived permanently in the lake, although it was only 10 feet deep or less. The lake became a stop for migrating birds, and some became permanent residents. The aquatic birds, especially ducks and geese, were attracted to the lake in large numbers. (Oakland History Center, Oakland Public Library.)

The birds attracted hunters from the region who fired their shotguns, which annoyed the residents in mansions along the shore due to the noise and pellets hitting their homes. Samuel Merritt solved this problem in a unique way—he convinced the governor of California to declare the lake an official nature reserve protecting all animals in 1870. The lake became the first nature reserve in the United States. (Author photograph.)

In 1876, Samuel Merritt built the Italianate Victorian Camron-Stanford House on the west shore of Lake Merritt. Alice and William Walker Camron purchased and occupied the house from 1876 to 1877; the family was the first to live in the home. The David Hewes family next bought the home and lived there from 1877 to 1881. Other families later occupied the house, including Josiah Stanford from 1882 to 1903. Josiah was the brother of Leland Stanford, who founded Stanford University in 1885. The house is the last remaining Victorian home of the many built along the shores of Lake Merritt. Capt. John T. Wright Jr. (1826–1911) and his family last occupied the house from 1903 to 1907; he sold it to the City of Oakland in October 1907 for $40,000. The house then served as the Oakland Public Museum until 1965. It was listed in the National Register of Historic Places in 1972 and became a Designated Oakland Landmark on January 7, 1975. It is seen here in 1876, shortly after it was first occupied. (Cameron Stanford House.)

The Twelfth Street Bridge and dam in Oakland attracted business as travel to the east side of Lake Merritt increased. Lake View Cottage, at 15 Twelfth Street on the south edge of the bridge, appears in this photograph inscribed "Souvenir of Fourth of July 1895." Lake View Cottage was an inn with an adjacent restaurant and saloon. The cottage served as an expansion of an existing restaurant, Bellevue du Rendez-vous de Chasse, which became commonly known as "House of Blazes," adapted from the owner's name. The resort as shown sat on pilings over San Antonio Creek on the south edge of the Twelfth Street dam. Business declined when the Eighth Street Bridge opened. (Oakland History Center, Oakland Public Library.)

The people of Oakland always appreciated their public libraries (above). The Oakland Library Association was established in 1868 with Mayor Samuel Merritt as president. Oakland poet Ina Coolbrith (1842–1928) was librarian from 1874 to 1892. Jack London and Isadora Duncan were self-educated chiefly in the library under Coolbrith's tutelage. The California Collection, focused on state history, was started by assistant librarian Mabel Thomas in 1921. Improved facilities, additional books, and a card catalog were added to the library later. In 1951, at the new main library, the California Collection with its books and materials became the California Room. The name was changed to the Oakland History Room in 1978 and to Oakland History Center in 2019. The main library (below) moved near Lake Merritt in 1951. It now has 16 branches. (Both, Oakland History Center, Oakland Public Library.)

Adams Point on the eastern shore of Lake Merritt was part of a larger estate owned by Edson Adams, for whom the point and neighborhood were named. The estate included not only the point, but the slopes of the hills to the east. His family did not live on the land; it was used to plant crops on the flat lands of the point. Later, a golf course was established near Adams Point on the current site of Lakeside Park. The golf clubhouse was built in 1885 and served chiefly the wealthy men of Oakland. After Adams died in 1888, his son, a banker also named Edson, inherited the land. He did little with the property, but Oakland had ideas of developing it into a public park with boulevards and pathways around the lake. In 1909, the city moved to acquire the land by eminent domain. Adams then sold the property. By 1912, the entire estate, except the point and Lakeside Park, was subdivided and sold. (Oakland History Center, Oakland Public Library.)

The Tubbs Hotel (above) was opened by Hiram Tubbs (1824–1897) in 1871 southeast of Lake Merritt in Brooklyn, which was incorporated into Oakland a year later. With 200 rooms occupying a city block and enclosed by landscaped surroundings with big trees, it was the largest structure in Oakland. Tubbs became rich in San Francisco manufacturing ropes and cordage for ships and mining. Tubbs was born in Concord, New Hampshire; ran a hotel in Boston; and came to San Francisco in 1853. He purchased land, developed a rail system, and promoted the Mountain View Cemetery in Oakland. The hotel was the venue for wealthy residents and visitors to Oakland. Its business slowed as Oakland, across Lake Merritt, grew; it burned down in 1893. Tubbs built his home across from the hotel near the Twelfth Street Bridge (below). (Both, Oakland History Center, Oakland Public Library.)

Dr. Samuel B. Merritt died in 1890 at age 68 after an active life in Oakland. He died where he lived, in a house he built just a block away from Lake Merritt on Jackson Street and Fourteenth Street. Said to be the wealthiest man in Oakland, Merritt left an estate estimated to be worth up to $3 million. Unmarried his entire life, he had no close relatives, but he left plans for a medical college and hospital to be built in his name. They were opened in 1909 and still serve the people of Oakland. His mausoleum, a miniature of the Mausoleum of Halicarnassus (one of the Seven Wonders of the Ancient World), was constructed on Millionaires Row in Mountain View Cemetery with views of Oakland and San Francisco Bay. Other historic figures of those cities are also interred along Millionaires Row. In 1933, the staff of Samuel Merritt Hospital placed a plaque to Merritt reading, "Physician, shipmaster, philanthropist, Regent of the University of California, mayor of Oakland, founder of Samuel Merritt Hospital." (Author photograph.)

By 1889, the margins of Lake Merritt had grown, with mansions, houses, and activities like swimming, fishing, and boating. The shoreline of the lake was still controlled by property owners who lived there. Parts of the lakeside had been planted with trees, but the shorelines were mostly left natural. No special embankments were in place to prevent erosion or slumping, although some owners had armored the edges with intercalated rocks. (Both, Oakland History Center, Oakland Public Library.)

The homes were widely spaced, at least in places on the east side, and a road was constructed and landscaped. The banks of the lake were cemented over to prevent erosion and make access to the water easy without the mud. (Library of Congress.)

By 1880, Oakland's population had grown to 34,555, on its way to 48,682 by 1890. Developers were pleased to build homes for people. Lake Merritt, too, was being developed around its edges and was a more desirable place for homes, with sewage partly controlled by disposal through pipes into San Francisco Bay. (Oakland History Center, Oakland Public Library.)

Four

INNOVATIONS

The development of Lake Merritt went hand in hand with that of the city of Oakland. Everyone had innovative ideas about what to do at the lake, in the lake, or with the lake, which benefitted from all the attention. A unique and dynamic body of water, the lake was previously a tidal slough with mudflats and seagrass. Innovations started when the first people built their shell mounds next to the lake's predecessor. And so, in modern times, modifications in many ways made the lake a completely human construct, except for the tides that come and go daily. These innovations started in 1868 and have been continuous to the present time. Dredging, roads, boating facilities, art works, museums, flood controls, a pump house to supply water for firefighting, recreational facilities, parks and greenbelts, and even rocks from the hills above Oakland were added to the lake and its surroundings. These aimed to improve the lake to make it a place people can enjoy, but it is not natural. The natural features of the earlier lakes were unattractive and would be considered so today as well. A human-made lake requires constant attention, maintenance, and innovation.

Lake Merritt attracted Oakland residents to build homes along its shores in the late 1800s and early 1900s. These were torn down beginning in the 1920s and replaced by apartments, businesses, churches, and government buildings. All this activity required roads around the lake that had to be reconfigured, particularly in the mid-1900s. Attractive public parks, greenbelts, and places of interest were added along the shorelines. The last major efforts to modify the lake and its shorelines came in the first two decades of the 21st century with the publicly supported Measure DD, which devoted $198 million to improve the lake, parks, and other city features used by residents of Oakland. The future of Lake Merritt looks terrific, but future dynamics will require careful planning and even greater innovation by the city and its citizens.

California was poorly prepared for public health emergencies when in 1900, the plague broke out in San Francisco, apparently transmitted by rats leaving ships from Honolulu that tied up at city docks. It soon spread to Oakland, which was one of the worst impacted cities in the state; more than 5,000 people were quarantined. Inspectors searched incoming ships at Oakland ports for rats, and hunters were dispatched all over Oakland, including Lake Merritt and surroundings, to shoot rats and squirrels. Henry Gage, governor of California, pushed by railroad and business interests, denied the presence of plague in the Bay Area, thus further hampering the struggle to eliminate it. The plague continued to infect people across the Bay Area, including Oakland, through the 1906 earthquake and fire in San Francisco. Oakland had no health care facilities, so people were treated at home. The plague reemerged in Oakland as late as 1919, killing 12 people at the same time that the flu pandemic spread throughout the city. (Library of Congress.)

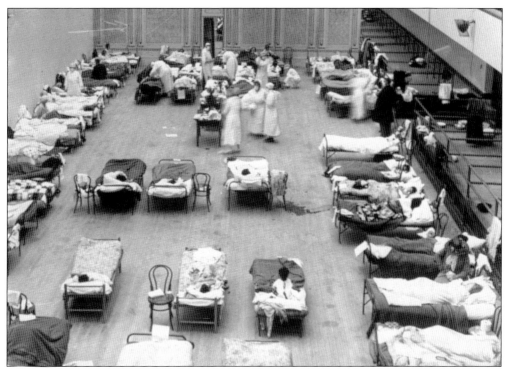

The 1918 flu pandemic severely impacted Oakland. Three flu cases appeared in September; by October 26, a total of 3,500 were reported. Public places like theaters, schools, churches, and Lake Merritt were closed on October 18. Nurses and medical supplies were lacking. The Oakland Auditorium at the lake was turned into an emergency hospital with 80 beds. Patients, mostly poor, were cared for by American Red Cross nurses (above), who also made masks (below). At one time, four patients were admitted every hour. Prisoners set up the auditorium and later buried the dead. Masks were mandated, with fines of $5 to $100 and jail sentences for those without one. Some citizens objected and were arrested. No flu vaccines existed then; 1,300 people died, but the worldwide death toll was 17–100 million. (Both, Oakland History Center, Oakland Public Library.)

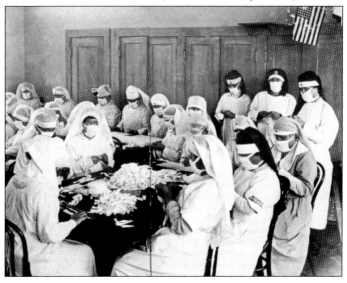

Earthquakes on the Hayward Fault and the San Andreas Fault occasionally rip through Lake Merritt and Oakland. No damage to the undeveloped lake was reported in 1865 or 1868. During the 1906 San Francisco earthquake (approximately 7.9 magnitude on the San Andreas Fault), the lake's shore slumped, as seen here. (California Historical Society.)

The 1906 San Francisco earthquake caused damage to brick buildings in Oakland and along the lakefront. Unlike San Francisco, Oakland had no fires. The destruction and fire in San Francisco caused people to evacuate across the bay to Oakland. Refugees were assisted with provisions and campsites on Adams Point at the northeast end of Lake Merritt. (Oakland History Center, Oakland Public Library.)

The Pergola, a landmark at the head of the eastern arm of Lake Merritt, is a picturesque, open structure with vines, columns, lattices, and a roof that shades a walking path (above). It is enjoyed by walkers, sitters, bird-watchers, and those who like to look at the lake's vistas, and it is a meeting place. Designed by Walter Reed in 1913, it has two pergolas (columns with roofs) separated by a central loggia and each ending in a smaller loggia. A boat landing faces the water on the southern side (below). Originally, the Pergola was called El Embarcadero because small boats used to land there to load products. That name was dropped, although the short road in front of the Pergola is still called El Embarcadero. (Above, Oakland History Center, Oakland Public Library; below, author photograph.)

Besides the boat landing at the Pergola, another landing was built in 1918 on the southeastern side of Lake Merritt at Eighteenth Street. The concrete landing has a broad, flat platform with stairs leading into the water and attractive walls and lampposts along the edges. It has remained in good condition and is used by pedestrians, boaters, and dancers. The Lindy Dance Club has held regular dance parties, known as Lindy by the Lake, on the boat landing. It is also a good place to view the lake and the city of Oakland on the other side. Note the homes along the southeastern shore. (Oakland History Center, Oakland Public Library.)

The apartment building at 1800 Lakeside Avenue (above) was constructed in 1909, one of the first apartment structures on the eastern side of Lake Merritt still in use. Its unique peaked roofs distinguish it from other buildings. The 1940 photograph shows the building and the realignment of Lakeshore Avenue (left), Eighteenth Street (in front of the building), Second Avenue (lower right), and Athol Avenue (right edge of the building). The intertidal zone at low tide near Eighteenth Street (right) reveals larger rocks, gravel, sand, shells, and green filamentous algae. A line of foam results from small waves striking the shore and mixing air with organic material in the water. In the distance is the boat landing. The edges of the lake are cemented to prevent erosion and slumping. (Above, Oakland History Center, Oakland Public Library; right, author photograph.)

McElroy Fountain was erected in 1911 in Lakeside Park to memorialize John E. McElroy (1870–1909), four-time Oakland city attorney who died at age 39 from pneumonia. He led the acquisition of Oakland's waterfront from the Southern Pacific Railroad and developed Oakland's first playgrounds. Designed by Douglas Tilden and constructed for $14,000, it is a magnificent structure made of Georgia white marble. It is Oakland Landmark No. LM 95-77. (Oakland History Center, Oakland Public Library.)

In Lake Merritt Gardens stands the Esterbrook Bird Fountain, a gift to the city from Nettie Esterbrook in 1914. Designed to allow birds to bathe, the fountain also serves as a centerpiece for the Mediterranean Garden, where pathways meet and radiate out. The fountain was made in Italy of white Carrara marble and sits atop three platform steps. (Author photograph.)

Francis Cutting (1834–1913), a California businessperson, began his career in Boston but came west in 1856 by ship to Panama, crossed the isthmus, and went on to San Francisco. In 1858, Cutting partnered with A.D. Baker, who produced cider, vinegar, and condiments, to operate a canning company (Baker & Cutting) and a glassworks factory. Cutting assumed the businesses, expanded the canning to the West Coast and Alaska, and operated a tin can manufacturing company, becoming the first to use them to preserve food. He shipped products to the East Coast, Europe, and Asia. One of Cutting's many labels, this one from the 1910s, is shown here. His company later became the Del Monte Company. Involved in shipping, banking, railroads, and other ventures, Cutting's primary interest was religion. In 1897, he married a recent divorcee, Sarah Abbie Kendall, who had property on Lake Merritt. Together, they built a showpiece mansion called Lakeside Terrace with grounds extending to the lake. Cutting died in 1913 of diabetes, and his ashes and Sarah's were buried in an unmarked plot in Mountain View Cemetery. (The Labelman.)

Several years after Francis Cutting's death, the City of Oakland purchased his estate. Henry Snow (1869–1927), a big game hunter, had a collection of mounted African animals that he offered to the city in the 1920s if a museum could be built to house them. Mayor John Davie believed that Snow's collection could be the foundation of a natural history museum and proposed that Cutting's mansion be used as the Snow Museum to exhibit the collection. Henry Snow accepted the proposal, and the building was filled with his collection, the precursor of the natural history section of the Oakland Museum. The property also had a small zoo that was later moved to Oakland Hills where it formed the basis for the city's zoo. The house is gone now, torn down in the 1960s. For a time, it appeared that a large convention-type hotel would be built there, but open space advocates prevailed, and Cutting's land remains as Snow Park across Lakeside Drive from Lake Merritt. (Oakland History Center, Oakland Public Library.)

In the 1960s, the Snow Museum was closed, and the mansion was razed. After discussion, the city constructed Snow Park on the small parcel. It now contains a playground, an enclosed toddler area, picnic areas, and landscaped grounds with big trees, green grass, and even a putting green remaining from a design of the 1960s. The park is considered by locals to be a great place to hang out in the heart of downtown Oakland; the space dates to the city's founding as its first cemetery. Geese seem to like Snow Park too, and their droppings are everywhere. The park was renovated under the city's Measure DD; it reopened in 2019. A special feature included in that project is the Makkewekes "rain garden" sculpture by WOWHAUS; it is tough to describe but presented as "an homage to Lake Merritt's restoration and a harkening of the return of native fauna." It looks like part shark, part ray, and part ichthyosaur hiding in the tall grass. The name, however, means "sea monster" in an Ohlone language. (Andrew Alden.)

August Schilling (1854–1934), of spice fame, came to San Francisco from Bremen, Germany, in 1870. Employed at J.A. Folger & Co., the coffee and spice firm, in 1875 he was made a partner in the company, which was renamed Folger, Schilling and Co. Together with George F. Volkmann, he founded the A. Schilling spice company. The Schillings bought land on Lake Merritt for a country home and gardens. They owned the property next to Francis Cutting from the 1880s until 1919 and erected an elegant mansion. Schilling Gardens, open to the public from 1890 to 1912, consisted of an exquisite collection of various plants and flowers growing down to the edge of Lake Merritt. In the 1920s, the estate was demolished to make room for large apartment buildings. (Both, Oakland History Center, Oakland Public Library.)

The Edoff Bandstand (right) was constructed from 1918 to 1920 near the beach on Glen Echo Arm. It is easily seen from across the arm (below). Paul Steindorff, the first musical director (1912–1917) of the Oakland Municipal Band, promoted a bandstand for Lake Merritt with a design similar to one in Milan, Italy. Funding was provided by a $2,000 donation by friends of James Edoff, past president of the board of park commissioners, with costs totaling $55,000. It was built of marble and limestone by European stonecutters. Closed from 1989 to 1999 due to damage from the Loma Prieta Earthquake, it was repaired with $1.5 million from the Federal Emergency Management Agency and Measure I-Life Enrichment Facilities bond funding. During this time, the Oakland Municipal Band played outside the bandstand. It is Oakland Landmark No. 9945, designated in 1979. (Both, author photograph.)

Alameda County has had courthouses in three communities. In 1875, the courthouse was moved to Oakland where it remained in Washington Square, even in disrepair, until it was razed in 1949. A new courthouse opened September 6, 1936, on an entire city block overlooking Lake Merritt. The building can be recognized by its impressive large base and tower from everywhere in or near Lake Merritt. It was built in the Moderne architectural style using reinforced concrete covered by California granite and terra-cotta. The lobby, open to the public, contains large marble murals depicting Alameda County's history by artist Marian Simpson of Berkeley and sculptor Gaetano Duccini of San Francisco. The building houses the Superior Courts of Alameda County. The first two floors hold offices, courtrooms are on the third through eighth floors, and the district attorney's office is on the ninth floor. The 10th and 11th floors house up to 100 inmates in the county jail. An observation cupola flanked with eagles crowns the building 200 feet above its base. (Oakland History Center, Oakland Public Library.)

People may have swum in San Antonio Slough, at least at high tide, and its creek for thousands of years and in Lake Merritt and its channel since 1869. The Ohlone, who had several shell mounds along the slough and creek, surely swam there starting around 4,000 years ago. It was also popular among Oakland residents in the late 1800s and 1900s. This 1905 photograph shows over 60 people swimming or lying on the grassy shore or slopes at the beach on the east side of Glen Echo Arm. However, swimming or bathing in the lake is now unlawful, although some occasionally do it. It is also unlawful to bathe or swim in Lake Merritt Channel or the Oakland Harbor without wearing a proper bathing suit. The channel shoreline has been modified with paths and beaches, so swimming is possible. (Oakland History Center, Oakland Public Library.)

A hidden history lies in the center of the Lake Chalet Restaurant housed in the old city boathouse: the federal Works Progress Administration's boat dock. During the Great Depression (1929–1941), the WPA initiated projects in Oakland, building a boat dock in the late 1930s adjacent to the city boathouse. The dock was made of wooden planks supported by pilings that deteriorated over time, but it was rebuilt as necessary. The dock was later placed between the wings of the old boathouse. In 2009, the Lake Chalet Restaurant opened and used the dock as a platform for a popular outside bar and dining area with scenic views of the lake. The photograph at left shows the end of the platform with the planks and pilings; the one below shows it occupied by diners. Both images were taken in 2022. (Both, author photograph.)

Lake Merritt was recognized officially as America's first wildlife refuge in 1870 by the State of California. In 2020, the 150th year of the refuge was celebrated at Adams Point near the Bird Islands. Bird Islands, seen here from 210 feet in the air, were constructed over time with soil from excavations (1920 or so) and sediment dredged at the western end of Lake Merritt (1923). John Davie, mayor of Oakland, wanted to promote the birds' welfare, so he constructed a 20,000 square-foot island he called Duck Island but which his opponents called "Davie's Folly." Not everyone was enamored with the ducks and geese that pooped all over the parks. Nevertheless, the islands accommodate the safe nesting and resting of the birds that migrate or stay at the lake. The islands are roped off to keep boats from disrupting the birds, and people must stay at least 50 feet away. Lakeside Park and the wildlife refuge were also designated Oakland landmark and heritage sites on July 8, 1980. (Michael Kozuch.)

An oil spill in 1915 from ships in the harbor floated into Lake Merritt, where it coated swimming birds with oil. Residents of Oakland tried to clean the ducks and demanded that the birds be saved. The city bought grain and fed the birds in a freshwater duck pond on Adams Point. Large crowds (above) gathered to watch the feeding of the ducks and other birds. The birds became accustomed to the morning and afternoon feedings announced by a ringing bell that signaled the birds and kids and their families to hurry to the pond to eat or to watch. Paul Covel, the lake's naturalist, remarked, "The daily afternoon feeding at the fresh-water pool has become the city's biggest free attraction." (Both, Oakland History Center, Oakland Public Library.)

Ducks, geese, and other water birds, both residents and migrants to Lake Merritt, may be found anywhere in the lake (above), but they are most abundant at the pond (right) on Adams Point, on the Bird Islands in the Trestle Glen Arm, or on the shores and grass of Lakeside Park. Mayor James Davie, who had assumed the birds' care in the 1920s with his Bird Islands, duck pond, and boat barriers, decided to band or tag the birds so they could be tracked. The city council approved it over some criticism and authorized the parks department to do it. The US Biological Survey stepped in and engaged E.W. Ehman, a local businessman, in 1926 to fix tags on the birds, keep records, and file reports. (Above, Oakland History Center, Oakland Public Library; right, author photograph.)

Lake Merritt's Necklace of Lights (above), a chain of lights on 126 lampposts around the lake, was installed in 1925 and was lit for the first time on August 27, 1925, during the Dons of Peralta Water Festival. Each lamppost was funded by an organization or an individual, acknowledged with an attached plaque like the one at left. The Necklace of Lights was illuminated every night until 1941, when they were extinguished to comply with blackout requirements during World War II. After the war, the light posts were removed, most were sold to China, and the rest were put in storage in Oakland. The Lake Merritt Breakfast Club refurbished the Necklace of Lights and relit it in 1985. Eleven more posts were added in 2008. On May 3, 1985, the Necklace of Lights was designated Oakland Landmark No. LM 85-39. (Both, Jim Carleton.)

The boats on Lake Merritt in the late 1880s provided opportunities for sailing and rowing (above). The Oakland Women's Rowing Club, formed in 1916, accepts women over the age of 50 to row for fun and exercise. They row whaleboats while dressed in their blue and white uniforms, as shown below in 1922 at the Lake Merritt Municipal Boathouse. Although powerboat racing was once popular, powerboats are no longer allowed on the lake. Boat racing still takes place on Lake Merritt but only with rowing crew boats. These are housed in the boat areas of the Lake Chalet building and docks. They are sponsored and run by the Lake Merritt Rowing Club, which anyone can join, to take part in novice, recreational, and competitive programs. (Both, Oakland History Center, Oakland Public Library.)

Leisure and recreational boating take place on Lake Merritt by individuals, in rental boats, and in courses. Private boathouses provided services in the 1800s (above), and the City of Oakland has been supportive of them since the early 1910s with the establishment of the old boathouse as part of the Pumphouse No. 1 water supply building, the boat landings at the Pergola in 1913 and Eighteenth Street in 1914, and the Oakland Boating Center at Adams Point. (Oakland History Center, Oakland Public Library.)

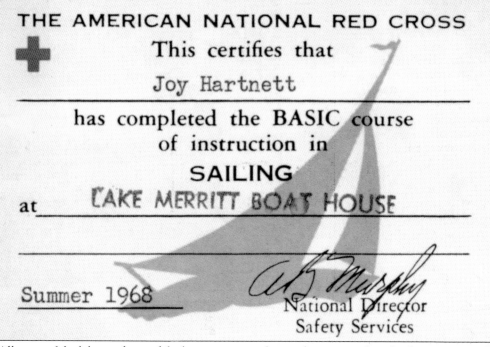

THE AMERICAN NATIONAL RED CROSS

This certifies that

Joy Hartnett

has completed the BASIC course of instruction in

SAILING

at LAKE MERRITT BOAT HOUSE

Summer 1968

National Director
Safety Services

All parts of the lake can be used for boating except the northeast arm where birds are protected. Some people took Red Cross sailing classes at the Lake Merritt boathouse and are still proud to show their certification cards. (Joy Hartnett.)

Boats—small sailboats, rowboats, sculls, and gondolas—were always important at Lake Merritt. Powerboats were used and raced from the 1920s until the 1980s but were banned because they caused disruptions to residents and the birds. The residents near Lake Merritt generally welcomed the powerboat races, particularly on the Fourth of July when skydivers landed in the lake and fireworks were displayed at night. (University of Southern California.)

The National Stock Outboard Championships were held here in 1952, with 50 loudspeakers around the lake. Men and women from 20 states raced; there were 202 entries. Marilyn Donaldson of Ohio took first place in a stock runabout race. Fifteen-year-old Dean Chenoweth from Ohio won three national titles in hydroplane and runabout races. Chenoweth had a storied career but died in a 175-mile-per-hour hydroplane crash in 1982. (Author's collection.)

National **STOCK OUTBOARD** *Championships*

• **LAKE MERRITT** • **OAKLAND, CALIFORNIA** •
September 20-21-22, 1952 • **Official Program**

On the east side of Lake Merritt, the Italian-style Cleveland Cascade climbs up the hill between residential buildings. Designed by landscape architect Howard Gilkey and developed in 1923, terraces, lit in colors at night, had water cascading down to the lake at the street below. The water was stopped during World War II. The structure was damaged, and weeds grew everywhere. (Oakland History Center, Oakland Public Library.)

The Cleveland Cascade continued to deteriorate until 2003, when neighborhood residents mobilized to restore it. A year later, plants, rather than water, were established in each of the bowls to resemble a cascade. Vegetation near the bowls and the stairs was restored too. The Cleveland Cascade is now a park. (Author photograph.)

The Veterans Memorial Building, opened in 1926, was among a number of outstanding structures designed by Oakland architect Henry H. Meyers. The building memorializes all veterans but especially those of the Spanish-American War of 1898. The building holds an auditorium, rooms for socializing or meetings, and offices. It is across Grand Avenue from the Glen Echo Arm. A torpedo port sits on the grounds. (Author photograph.)

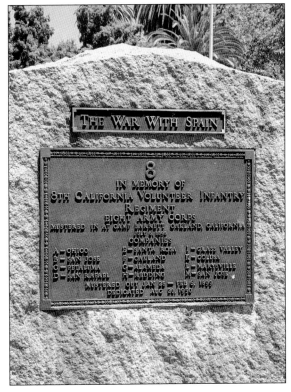

The Veterans Memorial Building site was donated to Oakland in 1903 by the estate of Edson Adams, an early founder of the city. It extends across Glen Echo Creek, where a plaque honors the veterans of the 8th Regiment of California Volunteers in 12 companies from 11 Northern California cities that mustered in on July 6, 1898, for the war with Spain. (Author photograph.)

The USS *Maine* (above), an American battleship, exploded and sank in Havana Harbor, Cuba, on February 15, 1898, initiating the Spanish-American War. Subsequent investigations concluded that it was either blown up purposely or that a coal dust fire exploded the munitions on the ship. The sinking became a cause for the Spanish-American War with the slogan, "Remember the *Maine*! To hell with Spain!" (Library of Congress.)

One of the *Maine's* four torpedo ports was given to the city of Oakland as a memorial. It was set in concrete in Lakeside Park in 1916. It remained there until May 2011, when it was stolen by men who tried to sell it for scrap. Luckily, it was recovered, and the torpedo port is now mounted in front of the Veterans Memorial Building across from Lake Merritt. (Author photograph.)

752 Piedmont Bath House, Oakland, California.

From 1891 to 1927, Piedmont Baths, an ornate Victorian-style bathhouse (above), stood at the intersection of Bay Place and Vernon Street, now the site of a Whole Foods store, about a block north of Glen Echo arm of Lake Merritt. A group of wealthy men, mostly from San Francisco, originated the idea and organized its development. Enormously popular and costing only 25¢, a large pool, 20 different baths, including Turkish and Russian, saline or fresh water hot tubs, and massages as well as a café were available. The central swimming pool was 70 by 120 feet with diving boards and trapezes along its sides. Water for the bathhouse was pumped from the bottom of either Lake Merritt or the Oakland Estuary depending on the tides. The water was heated to 212 degrees by a steam engine in the adjacent Oakland Cable Car plant. Because of fears of illness, the water ran through a series of filters. In spite of these precautions, a few people got sick, and some died. Piedmont Baths was finally destroyed in a huge fire in 1927. It was never rebuilt. (Oakland History Center, Oakland Public Library.)

Joseph Clarence Laney (1880–1948), a former newspaperman, urged that a central trade school be established to train students for jobs. He was elected to the Oakland Board of Education and its presidency in 1947. After his death in 1948, Central Trade Tech was renamed Laney Trade Tech and later Laney College. Laney College, begun in 1964 from predecessors started in 1927, moved to a new campus in 1970–1971 built on the site of the World War II Auditorium Village, shown above in 2022 with Lake Merritt Channel and the main campus of Laney College on the northwest side of the channel (right) while on the southeastern side (below), reached by a footbridge over the channel, is the Children's Center and the Laney College football stadium and baseball diamond. Laney College has 17,000 students. (Both, author photograph.)

Our Lady of Lourdes Catholic Church stands next to the Trestle Glen Arm and the Pergola. The parish celebrated its 100th anniversary in February 2022. The first mass and baptism were conducted in a parishioner's home in 1921. Property on the lake was purchased in 1923 for a school and auditorium that served as a temporary church until the present church was dedicated in 1961 and constructed from 1962 to 1963. The church, built in the Romanesque style of concrete and Italian marble, contains 12,300 square feet of space and a bell tower 110 feet tall. The church school was built in 1924 and closed in 1989 due to decreasing enrollment. The church serves an ever-changing, diverse parish. Recognizing this, plans were laid in the 1970s to change the church to better serve the parishioners by reorienting the altar and placement of the priests to face them. Completed in 1996, the changes and addition of an organ and pews cost over $1 million. Only three pastors have served in the church, all coincidentally from Ireland. (Jim Roach.)

On the east edge of Lake Merritt's Glen Echo Arm lies Children's Fairyland, a fantasy park for younger children. It opened in 1950 with the "Old Woman Who Lived in a Shoe" welcoming kids at the entrance (above, in 1953). Children's Fairyland was designed to entertain, amuse, and inspire children and their families with joy and in-person adventures represented by physical recreations of children's stories or sets. Those sets include tiny buildings, statues of characters (left), play equipment, creative play areas, and special children's adventures. Various kinds of animals can be seen, petted, and even ridden. Kids can also ride a small Ferris wheel, a merry-go-round, and other equipment and run through tunnels. The 10-acre site hosts gardens of trees and flowers wherever there is open space. Children's Fairyland operates with volunteers. (Above, Oakland History Center, Oakland Public Library; left, author photograph.)

Small children are particularly welcome at Children's Fairyland, where audiences are entertained by a variety of events, such as the Open Storybook Puppet Theater; special storytelling events (right, famed children's book author Marissa Moss reads to young girls in 1994); and storybook readings (below, in the 1950s). The performers were mostly volunteers. Displays of Oakland's history and diversity provide learning opportunities for kids and parents. Walt Disney, who visited Children's Fairyland in 1953, was fascinated by the park. He even hired volunteers from Children's Fairyland to help at Disneyland. (Both, Oakland History Center, Oakland Public Library.)

The Gardens at Lake Merritt (left) in Lakeside Park have been open to the public for 50 years. The park houses 17 specialized gardens on its seven-acre grounds. The gardens included are the Bay Friendly Demonstration, Bee Hotel, Bonsai, Community, Dahlia, Edible, Firescape, Japanese, Lakeside Palmetum, Lily, Mediterranean, Pollinator, Rhododendron, Sensory, Succulent (below), Torii Gate, and the Vireya Display. Each garden has particular plants or features. The Bee Hotel, for example, is focused on the processes involved in pollination. Taken together, the gardens exhibit a very large variety of unique and useful plants. The gardens are tended by volunteers and are open to the public for free. (Both, author photograph.)

The Bonsai Garden has over 250 bonsai with 100 trees usually exhibited on shelves. The idea for this garden goes back to bonsai enthusiasts in 1974. Funding for the garden took another 25 years and an agreement with the Golden State Bonsai Federation to approve a garden for Northern California. The City of Oakland agreed to place the Bonsai Garden in the Gardens at Lake Merritt, and it was finally opened to the public in November 1999. (Author photograph.)

The Lakeside Palmetum specializes in Mediterranean and cool-climate palms growing in its 0.6-acre plot. The collection was initiated and is maintained entirely by volunteers from the Northern California chapter of the International Palm Society, which started planting palms in 1982. More than 70 species live in the garden, ranging from quite large palm trees alongside smaller ones that grow well in Oakland's cooler, foggy climate. (Author photograph.)

Play areas for children are important at Lake Merritt. They are mostly in the Lakeside Park area. On the peaceful Bandstand Beach in the Glen Echo Arm ordinarily occupied by ducks sits the "Mid-century Monster," a unique fantasy play structure built in 1952. It was designed by Robert Winston, a teacher at Oakland's California College of Arts and Crafts, to provide a safe structure that stimulates the imagination of children. (Author photograph.)

The Mid-century Monster has no sharp edges to endanger climbers, and the sandy beach provides protection in a fall. Exactly what the monster is supposed to be is unknown, but it resembles a broken ship, a beached whale, the remains of a giant fish, or flotsam tossed onto the beach. Children have loved the Mid-century Monster for 72 years. (Author photograph.)

The Astro-Circle play area was constructed in Eastshore Park by the Oakland Department of Parks and Recreation and the Kiwanis Club in 1968. It was intended to excite kids about space. The play area had a flying saucer that kids could "fly" and the popular "Moon Cheese," which children could climb. (Author photograph.)

Although the spaceship was well used, it was removed in 2000 in part for safety reasons, and security mats were installed throughout the area, leaving a standard set of playground equipment with slides, swings, and a climbing structure. The play area is encircled by stones (one is shown here) reused from the 1871–1895 Oakland High School. (Andrew Aldan.)

Most monuments in the parks at Lake Merritt have been donated by individuals who wanted to honor another person. Two memorials along Bellevue Avenue in Lakeside Park honor children killed in Alameda County (left) and Sallie Rutherford Thaler (below). The *Children's Memorial Statue* near Adams Point remembers 433 children who have died violently since the 1990s. The statue, designed by Dennis Smith of Utah, was dedicated on April 22, 2016, amid controversy about its appropriateness in a park, especially near Children's Fairyland. Irwin Luckman designed the fountain memorializing Sallie Rutherford Thaler (1888–1958). A longtime member of Native Daughters of the Golden West and a grand trustee of the order and grand secretary, she loved nature and Lake Merritt. At the dedication ceremony in 1961, Mayor Clifford Rishell accepted the fountain on behalf of the city. (Both, author photograph.)

Festivals and concerts have been held at the auditorium, amphitheater, the gardens, on the lake itself, near the Pergola, and on parkland along the lake. They began as early as the early 1900s and have continued to be offered by independent organizers and the city itself. Thousands of people attend the open-air events, which include vendors selling food and wares. Concerts were popular, with an assortment of bands and singers, some very highly praised. Bassist-director Miles Perkins came with outstanding world-famous artists to the Festival at the Lake on October 11, 1997 (above), where dancers were a prominent feature (right). These festivals ended in 1997 due to organizational and financial constraints. (Both, Oakland History Center, Oakland Public Library.)

Henry J. Kaiser (1882–1967), born in New York, migrated west to Washington state in 1906. He established a construction company and began a lifelong role in the industry, constructing buildings, dams, Liberty ships in World War II, and automobiles, among other things, and started the Kaiser Permanente Health program, the largest in the United States. He eventually owned more than 100 companies and accumulated a fortune worth over $2.5 billion. Kaiser made Oakland his world headquarters; its home was on the top floor of the Kaiser Tower. This sculpture of Henry Kaiser is part of the *Champions for Humanity* monument in Henry J. Kaiser Park, five blocks west of his buildings on Lake Merritt. Four large statues in the monument honor and highlight the greatest and most influential international peace figures ever known, such as Mother Teresa, Abraham Lincoln, and Nelson Mandela. The Kaiser figure is on one of the large sculptures between Joyce Taylor (on his left) and Mary Ann Taylor and Joaquin Miller (on his right), all Oakland celebrities. Large plaques commemorate their work toward freedom, equality, and peace. (Author photograph.)

From 1949 to the 1950s, the roads at the Twelfth Street Bridge over Lake Merritt Channel underwent a reconfiguration to improve traffic. The construction took place in front of the Oakland Auditorium and the Alameda Courthouse. The lakeside (at left) was left without improvement, with just an intertidal zone from the bridge to the greenbelt on the western side of the lake. (Oakland History Center, Oakland Public Library.)

When completed, a complex of roads crossed the channel spreading out in both eastern and western approaches that wound through the historical buildings: the Oakland Library at lower left, the Alameda Courthouse at center, and the auditorium out of sight to the right. Pedestrians have little room to pass through this complex. (Oakland History Center, Oakland Public Library.)

After a white woman encountered two black men barbecuing at the lake and called the police, BBQ'n While Black, shown here in 2018, became a series of annual events. Black people have long held various events and celebrations at Lake Merritt, especially since a Black Panther rally in 1968. Thousands have gathered in the parks for political and diversity rallies, festivals, concerts, parties, family gatherings, group barbecues, and vendors selling a wide variety of items. These events have brought the community together and are fun and enjoyed by everyone. (Michael Short/San Francisco Chronicle.)

Dragon boat celebrations are a 2,500-year-old Chinese tradition. Lake Merritt was part of that from 2009 to 2020 as the Northern California International Dragon Boat Festival took place here. Organized by the Northern California Dragon Boat Association and Oakland Renegades Dragon Boat Club, the boaters celebrated Chinese culture with performances, sports, food, crafts, art, kids' activities in Dragon Land, and dragon boat races. This photograph is from a race in 2017. (Jimmy Chan.)

Over 130 world-class dragon boat teams from various countries compete, drums beating, for honors sponsored by corporations, community groups, and other novice teams. Each boat is up to 40 feet long with a dragon bow figure and crewed by 20 paddlers, a drummer, and steersperson. Two boats from the 1970s deteriorated until they were hauled away; they were made of teak in Hong Kong. (Jimmy Chan.)

Flooding in the Lake Merritt area is a threat during large storms. It lies low, with streams bringing storm water from the East Bay hills, so it collects there faster than it can drain through the lake to the bay. Heavy rains also carry debris through storm drains into the lake. When the lake level rises above three feet, flooding begins. A huge storm in 1962 dropped 9.4 inches of rain in Oakland in 24 hours, causing the lake level to rise to 7.3 feet and filling the streets and neighborhoods around it. Stores and homes were flooded, and automobiles were disabled in the streets. This flood started a movement to build floodgates at the Seventh Street Bridge in the Lake Merritt Channel to control the water levels in the lake. (Both, Alameda County Public Works Agency.)

Lake Merritt flooded on New Year's Day 2023 due to a combination of heavy rains the previous day and night and high tides. Over 5.2 inches of rain fell at Lake Merritt, and more than 6 inches were recorded in the 4,650-acre watershed in the hills above the lake. The inflow raised the lake's level, causing it to overflow its banks onto the paths and parklands (above). At the Oakland Boathouse, water rose to the doorways (below), as this area is the lowest edge of the lake. Nothing was severely damaged, and the tide gates at the Seventh Street crossing were opened. The lake drained at low tide through its channel into the San Francisco Bay. Debris was swept both into and out of the lake. (Above, Adrian Cotter; below, Kerstin Firmin.)

Lake Merritt provides flood control by retaining overflow water. A flood control station with tidal gates 12 feet high and four powerful diesel pumps was constructed on Lake Merritt Channel at the Seventh Street Bridge in 1968 to avoid a repetition of the 1962 flood. The gates (above) are kept half open to allow water and wildlife to pass. When flooding threatens, the gates are opened to let water flow out (below) or closed to prevent high tides from entering. The pumps can lower lake levels before high tides, large inflows, or sudden inputs of water to the lake. The pumps are seldom used because the gates control water levels. When the gates are half open, insufficient inflow may occur to prevent low oxygen levels and the passage of wildlife to the lake. (Both, Adrian Cotter.)

Like in big cities everywhere, Lake Merritt is impacted by littering, pollution, vandalism, theft, and worse. Litter has long been a problem, starting in the earliest days of Oakland when sewage and garbage was disposed of in the slough and later the lake. Modern litter and pollution enter the lake from at least three sources: through the more than 60 storm drains, throwing of trash, or road runoff. The Lake Merritt Institute oversees volunteers who routinely clean debris from the water. Tagging surfaces with graffiti is common, but the city paints over it. Vandalism has occurred for a long time. Thefts have taken place too: in 1934, a motor from the Necklace of Lights was taken; in 2011, the *Maine's* torpedo port was stolen; and in 2013, a total of 40,000 feet of copper wire was gutted from the Necklace of Lights. (Above, Vida Pavesich; below, author photograph.)

Paul Frederick Covel (1908–1990) attended high school in San Diego, tended birds at the San Diego Zoo, then moved to New York City and worked on birds at the American Museum of Natural History, collecting them in Central America. He moved to Oakland, where he had jobs in the late 1930s to 1940s at Snow Museum, Oakland Museum, and Lake Merritt refuge; he also lectured on birds. Famous for his conservation efforts with wildlife and ecosystems in Oakland, he was appointed by the city as naturalist at Lake Merritt in 1948, the first city naturalist in the country. Roger Tory Peterson, famed birder, visited Covel in 1961 to see the birds (shown here at the lake). Covel designed exhibits in the Rotary Natural Science Center. Retiring in 1970 from the Oakland Department of Parks and Recreation, Covel wrote two natural history books—*People are for the Birds* and *Beacons along a Naturalist's Trail*—and several pamphlets, taught classes on the environment and natural history, and took trips to four continents to write and photograph natural history. (James Covel.)

This mid-1960s photograph taken by Harold Winder, a lake and park department gardener, shows the Rotary Natural Science Center in Lakeside Park. Renamed the Rotary Nature Center, it maintains and protects Lake Merritt and other open spaces in Oakland. Its building, designed by Paul Covel, was constructed in 1953. It houses educational and interpretive exhibits and provides natural science and urban wildlife presentations, field trips, and summer youth camps. (Oakland History Center, Oakland Public Library.)

The Rotary Nature Center is shown in 2023 surrounded by large trees and the eagle totem pole, erected in 1999. Eagle Helikinuva, of the Pacific Northwest Tsimshian Nation, carved the totem, which was blessed by the Inter-Tribal Friendship House. The pole welcomes people to the center and lake. Its icons celebrate Lake Merritt. Rotary Nature Center Friends, an all-volunteer community organization, supports interpretive education for all people of Oakland. (Author photograph.)

Jim Carlton, an Oakland teenager, stumbled on a cluster of marine tubeworms while exploring Lake Merritt in 1962. The worm originated in Australian waters and had spread to the lake from elsewhere in the world. This spurred Carlton's interest in the lake's biology, which prompted him to establish the Lake Merritt Biological Survey in his parents' house. He is shown above in his lab in 1968. His work on the lake's invasive species appeared in the *Oakland Tribune* and started his outstanding career in marine biology. Earning a doctorate from the University of California, Davis, Carlton became professor of marine sciences at Williams College in Massachusetts and was director of the Williams College–Mystic Seaport Ocean & Coastal Studies Program in Mystic, Connecticut, from 1989 to 2015. Carlton returned to Lake Merritt for research. His work on invasive species and modern extinctions garnered awards. He received the first US Interagency Recognition Award for work on marine species invasions, and the James T. Carlton Marine Science Center, a teaching and research facility at the Williams-Mystic Program, was named in his honor. It all began at Lake Merritt more than 60 years ago. (Lisa Carlton.)

Algae and marine plants grow profusely in clumps below the surface throughout Lake Merritt. When they die and fall to the bottom, their decomposition uses oxygen, and the oxygen levels of the water may decrease, killing fish and other life. A harvester is brought in to cut and remove them before they die. (Author photograph.)

The cuttings and other debris scooped up are dumped on a belt to move them to the rear of the harvester. This harvest is taken to shore at the boating center on Adams Point, where it is loaded onto trailers and taken to a local landfill. The harvester not only removes algae and plants, but also an assortment of animals that live among them like pipefish, snails, and sponges. (Author photograph.)

Non-native, invasive species have been introduced into Lake Merritt and the channel probably since foreign ships first came to the San Francisco Bay in 1769. The first documented introduced species, the smooth Atlantic soft-shell clam (pictured), came by railroad in the 1870s. Railcars were loaded with live oysters in New England, and those, along with other live species, were dumped into the San Francisco Bay. Sixty or more invasive species in the lake have been introduced on or in ships as larvae or adults. They include single-celled microscopic organisms, many different invertebrates, and fish. The Japanese littleneck clam with radiating ribs was introduced in the 1940s from Japan, as was a foraminiferan first recorded in 1982 in the East Bay and since found across the bay. A tubeworm came from Australia as it spread across the globe. Introduced microorganisms living in the water column (planktonic) are virtually unknown. Non-native species can cause ecological problems, such as excluding native species from their habitats, but these are not well-studied in Lake Merritt. (Author photograph.)

Besides birds, Lake Merritt hosts over 600 species of marine invertebrates and microorganisms, hundreds of fish (halibut, salmon, skates, rays, small sharks, and pipefish, seen at right), and an occasional sea lion or sea otter. Larger algae grow abundantly in the shallows, and microscopic algae, protozoans, and animals inhabit the bottom and water. Bacteria and viruses are present but have not been surveyed. The animals live in all parts of the lake and at all depths. (Author photograph.)

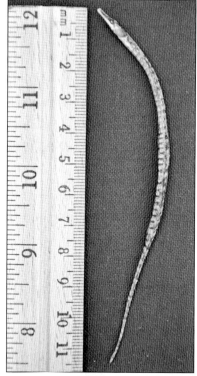

After reproduction, animal larvae swim or float in the water or larvae are introduced from the San Francisco Bay through Lake Merritt Channel. These colonize the water, muddy bottoms, rocks near the shore, and objects hanging in the water, where they grow into adults. The most obvious include nudibranches like the quarter-inch specimen pictured here, sponges, tunicates, clams, mussels, and others, which will settle on a panel hanging in the water. (Robin Gwen Agarwal.)

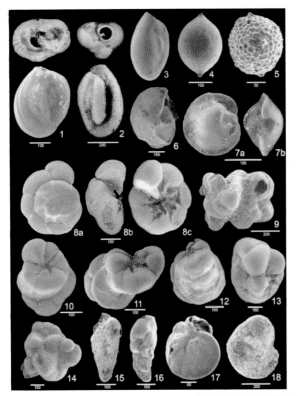

Microscopic organisms may be the most abundant and least understood organisms in Lake Merritt. Foraminifera (left), single-celled protozoans with shells of calcium carbonate or agglutinated sediment, live on the bottom and respond to changing conditions by growth or death of their populations. So do tiny animals, very commonly overlooked by visitors, like ostracods (below), which are also environmental indicators and are important in the lake's ecology. These are all sensitive to the varying salinity, temperature, and oxygen content of the lake. Larger animals may feed on these tiny organisms. The open water contains innumerable microscopic algae such as diatoms, dinoflagellates, and others that are important primary producers supporting larger animals that feed directly from the water or eat material deposited on the bottom of the lake. (Both, Ken Finger.)

In August 2022, thousands of fish and invertebrates died in the Bay Area, including Lake Merritt and its channel, with fish of all kinds gasping for air at the surface. Dead fish were stranded along the shores; the City of Oakland removed over 1,200 pounds of dead fish and other organisms and disposed of them in a landfill. Low oxygen levels, toxins from plankton, the decomposition of larger algae on the bottom depleting oxygen, and climate warming were all suggested as causes. Measurements by Katie Noonan revealed that oxygen at depth decreased to zero, the lowest she recorded for years, and was the immediate cause of animal deaths. Why the oxygen decreased has not been determined. A bloom of the microscopic algae *Heterosigma akashiwo* may have died and decomposed, depleting the oxygen. (Both, Damon Tighe.)

COVID hit Lake Merritt hard in 2020-2021. Activities were curtailed, and masks were required, although some users of the lake objected to these actions. These reactions were not new in Oakland. During the 1900-1906 plague and the 1918-1919 flu pandemic that infected citizens in large numbers, objections to official health measures were raised. Businesses and places of assembly were closed down, and people who chose not to wear masks in public were arrested and fined. Vaccines, however, were not available then, and it would be decades before those for flu, measles, polio, and a host of other viruses became available and saved millions of lives across the country. At Lake Merritt, events came back slowly, although masks were still required until 2022. With vaccinations available to anyone, field education resumed in 2022 with masks. (Katie Noonan.)

Lake Merritt suffers from problems associated with estuaries everywhere, although the lake has been reconstructed by residents and the city absent its mudflats and seagrass meadows. The inflow of dense, salty water at high tides fills the bottom of the lake, where it is covered by less dense freshwater floating at shallower depths. The salty water remains on the bottom, where dead plants, algae, and animals accumulate and decompose, using up oxygen and resulting in low to no oxygen in the bottom waters. The process creates smells and kills animals and plants that may live there or prevents those organisms from living on the bottom. At Lake Merritt, decorative fountains (pictured in 2006) were installed that are supposed to aerate the bottom waters, but that does not happen because the water sprayed into the air does not stay long enough to get oxygenated. The fountains stir the water from the bottom to the surface, which is helpful, but hundreds of fountains would be required to do that over the entire lake. Other solutions must be discovered. (Steven Gross.)

Lake Merritt faces challenges in the future because, as an estuary, it is vulnerable to rising sea levels caused by global warming. Of that warming, 90 percent goes into the oceans, causing expansion of seawater. The City of Oakland estimates the rise will be four feet by 2050 and nine feet by 2100. The four-foot rise would push the lake over neighboring roads and parklands. A nine-foot rise would flood neighborhoods and lakeside parks, and the lake would be five feet underwater. These estimates do not include increases from the melting and collapsing of glaciers in Greenland and Antarctica, which could raise oceans 30 feet or more, much like it was 125,000 years ago. At that time, Adams Point (pictured in 1890) and coastal areas around the bay were under water, flattened by erosion and deposits of alluvium that could be repeated in the future. Rises will increase tidal flooding, storm surges, erosion, and a rising salty water table and probably require moving communities to higher ground. Wise planning for rising sea levels will be essential. (Oakland History Center, Oakland Public Library.)

BIBLIOGRAPHY

Alden, Andrew. *Deep Oakland: How Geology Shaped a City.* Berkeley, CA: Heyday Books, 2023.

Allen, Annalee. *Oakland.* Charleston, SC: Arcadia Publishing, 2005.

Bagwell, Beth. *Oakland: The Story of a City.* Novato, CA: Presidio Press, 1982.

Bean, Lowell John. *The Ohlone Past and Present.* Menlo Park, CA: Ballena Press, 1994.

Burgess, Sherwood D. *The Water King: Anthony Chabot, His Life and Times.* Davis, CA: Panorama West Publishers, 1992.

Covel, Paul F. *People are for the Birds.* Oakland, CA: Western Interpretive Press, 1978.

Elliott, W.W. *Oakland and Surroundings Illustrated and Described showing its Advantages for Residence or Business.* Oakland, CA: W.W. Elliott, 1885. Marula Historical Reprint, Charleston, SC: Arcadia Publishing.

Harris, Alex. *Birds of Lake Merritt.* Berkeley, CA: Heyday Books, 2021.

Henning, Koford. *Dr. Samuel Merritt: His Life and Achievements.* Oakland, CA: The Samuel Merritt Hospital, 1938.

Lavoie, Steven. *Historic Photos of Oakland.* Nashville, TN: Turner Publishing Company, 2009.

Metz, Randal J. *Children's Fairyland.* Charleston, SC: Arcadia Publishing, 2016.

Nelson, N.C. "Shellmounds of the San Francisco Bay Region." *University of California Publications in American Archaeology and Ethnology. Vol.* 7, No. 4., 1909.

Ricketts, Edward F., Jack Calvin, Joel W. Hedgpeth, revised by David W. Phillips. *Between Pacific Tides.* Fifth Edition. Stanford, CA: Stanford University Press, 1992.

Rizzo-Martinez, Martin. *We Are Not Animals. Indigenous Politics of Survival, Rebellion, and Reconstitution in Nineteenth Century California.* Lincoln, NE: University of Nebraska Press, 2022.

Slone, Doris, with photographs by John Karachewski. *Geology of the San Francisco Bay Region.* Berkeley, CA: University of California Press, 2006.

Uhle, Max. "The Emeryville Shellmound." *University of California Publications in American Archaeology and Ethnology.* Vol. 7, No. 1, 1907.

Waiczis, Michael R. *Henry A. Snow and the Snow Museum of Natural History.* Oakland, CA. The Oakland Museum, 1983.

Williams, Jack S. *The Ohlone of California. The Library of Native Americans.* New York, NY: The Rosen Publishing Group, 2003.

DISCOVER THOUSANDS OF LOCAL HISTORY BOOKS
FEATURING MILLIONS OF VINTAGE IMAGES

Arcadia Publishing, the leading local history publisher in the United States, is committed to making history accessible and meaningful through publishing books that celebrate and preserve the heritage of America's people and places.

Find more books like this at
www.arcadiapublishing.com

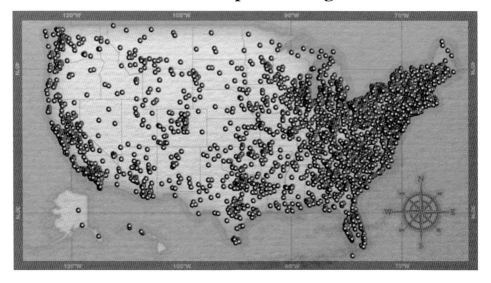

Search for your hometown history, your old stomping grounds, and even your favorite sports team.

Consistent with our mission to preserve history on a local level, this book was printed in South Carolina on American-made paper and manufactured entirely in the United States. Products carrying the accredited Forest Stewardship Council (FSC) label are printed on 100 percent FSC-certified paper.